MW01265045

Half Heard Voices

Bobbie Ward

before these hands
are stilled
and the world is stopped
will you
know me (then)
when there's nothing
here to keep you
(dis-believing)

Sharon—
It's what you
do that makes
your soul !

Love,
Bobbie
2012

Copyright 2012 by Bobbie Ward

All rights reserved under International and Pan-American Copyright Conventions. No part of this book may be used or reproduced in any manner whatsoever without written permission except in the case of brief quotations embodied in critical articles and reviews.

Photo & Cover Design
by Rania Rönntoft – Rania Maria Photography.
For additional information, please visit Rania's
website at www.raniamaria.eu

Manufactured and printed
in the United States of America

ISBN-13: 978-1470008901
ISBN-10: 1470008904

First Printing: February 2012

comes a time

there comes a time when time is lost
and dreams you dreamed before are done
when now is all the time you have
and this the you you've now become

there comes a day when days are past
and tomorrow waits your place to find
a path forever yours to know
was waiting for this perfect time

there comes a breath as none you've known
how sweet the taste of love you've kissed
how warm the touch of Summer sun
how long the grief for love you missed

there comes a voice of immortal calm
was there when first your heart could hear
when first your eyes were opened wide
a spirit came to hold you near

there comes a life when life is through
and moss grows smooth across your breast
when all that was - two dates recall
a granite page - of living rest

there comes a time when time is lost
though not this day would silence fall
were not this wondrous light returned
eternal life - this gift to all

yestersun

between the dawn and twilight creeps
some sunlight formed of amber hue
would find its way amidst the rain
a moment blessed - a life renewed

between the hours of dusk and set
how much of time we take to touch
how much we keep of all we find
how much of love is e'er enough

between the stars of melting blue
how many held our wishes near
how many fell beyond our grace
a sparkle lost - forever clear

between the set of yestersun
another rise would surely bring
how many dreams we left to sleep
how many prayers one angel sings

an ounce of time would weigh the same
tomorrow's sun - her task begins
were not for those who seek the truth
if wasted - ne'er would rise again

for yesterday is passed from view
and moments left unspent shall dry
as leaves once dusted from the oak
to wither 'neath tomorrow's sky

Here

I know you're here
I see your eyes-forever
green
your love on each horizon
the promise of days
between

I know you're here
how your touch this
moment slows
as near to heaven
I have held
within the silence grows

I know you're here
is that your kiss still on
my breath
the taste of every dream
we've shared
shall linger beyond my
death

I know you're here
memories fill these lonely
nights
the wonder born of
yesterday
shall be tomorrow's light

Unto Us

I hear your voice
far above the winter
storm
far above this prayerful
silence -
for this moment you were
born

I hear your voice
from a miracle was made
a light to pierce the
darkness
at creation's essence laid

I hear your voice
where wing-ed soldiers
ride
cloaked with all the faith
they need
to reach the northern
tide

I hear your voice
in vespers - crystal blue
a wave against
eternal shores
a storm resounding you

I hear your voice

Hell to pay

I am bruised
from the darkness
where sorrow lay sleeping
where anger and anguish
are laid next to dreams
what time has forgotten
the world left for nothing
e'er love have no meaning
to the night
in between

I am deaf
from the silence
of passion's retreating
one moment of grace
to shadows would fall
a point of surrender
what flickering madness
would burn through the
candle
in hope
for us all

I am lost
but immortal
my soul will remember
e'er seeds of tomorrow
be planted today
were branches grown
over
the storms will protect
me
would the rain
beat the morning
or declare
hell to pay

I am saved
but forsaken
by those without mercy
by those who bear
witness
my sins to confess
what lies are left wanting
the truth to redeem me
the blessing of pardon
e'er I be nothing
or less

wiser sun

what questions writ
an answer true
to melt beneath
a wiser sun
what storms were raged
before the rise
to grieve again
the past undone

what miracle
of life's delight
would warm beneath
immortal skies
reflecting light
tomorrow's birth
across the world
a new sunrise

eternity
this moment keeps
beyond the twilight
a dawn shall break
beyond the knowledge
a wiser sun
waits to rise
e'er souls awake

again

if given the words
could I write you a story
and spin you a truth
of lies I know well
then a thousand excuses
not one worth repeating
would you dare to remember
the choice I could tell

this place is my doing
my fate still becoming
when blinded by want
beyond mine to touch
so easy to see
now the way I neglected
a lifetime of blessings
a moment too much

what price would I pay
to change then the future?
to relive every second
my will to concede
to right every wrong
of this journey returning
life filled with purpose
this destiny seed

but now I must go
only one way is offered
back to the light
I betrayed in my youth
back to the giver
of life everlasting
beginning again
my story of truth

Rich with Rain

I want serenades
of evermore
and roses filled with dew
sweet ambrosia dusting
a tearful night
or two

I want silken sheets
two thousand count
and candles slowly burned
a night that lasts forever
a longing kiss
returned

I want purple dusks
and crimson dawns
and rainbows in between
the song a dove surrenders
to meadows evergreen

I want yellow sails
and ocean tides
to wash on endless shores
in waves of blue becoming
forever wanting more

I want words to fall
from where I slept
to pages rich with rain
a lifetime's breath
returned to life
in dreams we loved
the same

Beside

on distant plains
I walk beside
another life
I left behind
resolved no more
the past to keep
and yet his shadow
here resides

beside the wall
where oceans sleep
beneath a ragged
shade of shale
tumbled down
forever came
to meet with joy
her rushing swell

on southern winds
I sail apart
from all the past
I've lived and fought
I touch with wings
uncharted suns
were blackest moons
with stardust bought

these wings of light
they love the dawn
and kiss the sweetest
blush of sun
til twilight sweeps a purple sky
I'll walk beside
the past undone

hidden

how sweet the voice
of silence sings
in darkness
to the light
across a silken shoulder
once hidden
by the night

how light the touch
of longing falls
within a moonlight
glowed
to wash along
a lover's breast
was once a kiss
bestowed

how warm the breath
of loving sighs
in hours spent between
the edge of sunlight
dancing
in twilight
barely seen

coo

the white dove swelled
her battered breast
and cocked
her silver head
to hear
an ancient sound
of love returned
and dreams succumb
to restless fear

a sacred coo
of longing falls
to shake the snow
from branches bent
beneath the boughs
were calls of love
from feathered clouds
by loving spent

into the wind
her whisper flies
a tale of time
and battles won
the white dove wings
into the light
and spreads her wings
to greet the sun

11

play me the music

play me the music
was played
on that first morning
when breath became
immortal
and fell into the wood
play me the melody
of love
before they knew it
alone within the garden
blessed with light
eternal good

play me the music
that danced upon the
water
when sailed into the
sunrise
his search for distant
gold
play me the harmony
of dreams forever
wanting
a place no one imagined
a story
yet untold

play me the music
that floats
to fill a meadow

weaved between a
butterfly
a morning wing
embraced
play me the solitude
revealed in nature's
longing
born unto a clover green
resounding
heaven's grace

play me the music
was only heard by lovers
and kept beneath the
twilight
where music turns to
skin
play me the lullaby
no chord could ever
measure
pressed into a symphony
of silent still amen

play me the music

Butterfly dreams

Soft as feather down
clear as a summer rainbow
butterfly dreams come

Winds carry her home
across the days between
forever she loves

would your wings

would your wings forever
rise
and bear my wounded
soul above
would press about my
broken heart
and warm my cooling
brow with love

would your wings a
solace be
when all the world is
closing in
would you wrap around
my fears
and bring me home - to
live again

would your wings a
memory make
of all we've shared - a
tapestry
spun of silk to match
your flight
across this broken world
to me

would your wings forever
rise...

13

silence stills

silence stills a moment whispered
becomes a sigh
from longing sweet
greets the dawn with measured kisses
no words could e'er
their truth repeat
loving souls embrace the morrow
lift the clouds up off the sun
dry the dew
a senseless wonder
finds the two remain as one

in between the night and falling
all that is
our will to be
fills the shadows
a softness shifting
moves to light
a memory

Lexington

The way returned
was not the best,
though we were
by kindred minds -
by kindness found
and eyes of light -
A place remained
by truth defined.

Some comfort came
the darkness split,
as normal would
and normal is -
into a place
where strangers love -
Was grace reserved
for such as this?

I cannot say
what might have been,
or speak to fate -
another cost.
But mourn for friends
a moment shared -
another place -
our paths would cross.

Come of Age

I've come of age
a little bit late -
way past the point
I reached my prime...
My eyes now open
(sometimes I blink)
to what has been
and was never mine.

I've hit my knees
and stood up strong -
sometimes I thought
I never would.
I've seen the best
and worst of me
and know myself -
more right than good.

There is no flag
of surrender here -
no looking back
to sleepless nights.
I've marked my days
in blood and tears -
and know this breath
was worth the fight.

Do we ever lose
in letting go...
for only then
is our purpose met.
When comes the time
we find the truth -
in what we wished
and what we let.

Twas Me

I found the road
was left behind
and none the worse for
wear
or time -
and though the blooms
had fell to snow
there were no signs
of me to find...

Along the path
the vines had spread
and weaved a bridge
across my heart
had held above
the rising tides -
a place was meant
for me to start...

I cannot know
how long the days
between the last
breath and the first
but understand
that time was naught
for me to still
my longing thirst...

Where would I go -
or would I try
to find the way
back home to this
to know that home
was always me -
and what of love
twas me I missed.

More Than Roses

It's enough
that I remember
the way you said hello -
A smile was all I needed
to be sure of what I know
- that nothing is forever
but what we keep within.

As dear the pearl was
given
it is left to be again.

It's enough
that I've forgotten
what of hurt we said
goodbye -
beneath a blanket of
October
and a chilly autumn sky.

I don't need forever,
darling
to know what's in your
heart.
Were there words -
we must have found
them -
nothing but a place to
start.

It's enough
for my tomorrows,
what today I know is
real.
I don't need
a new assurance -
all I need is what I feel.

If that is all
that's left to keep me -
keep me well
it sure will do.

What I have is more than
roses -
what I have
is loving you.

You Loved the Best

Would that every sunrise
be a reminder of my love.
Every moment -
yours for waking
to the dream your fondest of.

Would that every memory
be the one
you loved the best -
every breath of life surrendered -
every longing truth confessed.

Would that this returning
be your testament to share -
every passing you remember -
every kiss you had to spare.

Would that this remembrance
be your purpose from the fall -
e'er the moments
you were witness
be a blessing to us all.

Would your wings
embrace the heavens
and press against the blue -
to love the world
beyond this world -
e'er I'll be loving you

.

The Maze

I wandered from the
maze
seeking solace
from the storm -
looking back into
tomorrow
to the night
from which I'd come.

There were days
without compassion -
my thirst deprived of
drink.
There were lies
consumed by questions
and thoughts
no one should think.

But I found
along my journey
what I knew right from
the start -
that love could not betray
me
for it lives
within my heart.

Though the roads
were always turning -
how I fought
you'll never know -
all the ways
I took in error -
tears remembered
to my soul.

It was only in the rising
above the maze
that is my life,
I could see
the truth mistaken -
every stumble -
every strife.

I can see the place I
faltered -
what of love
did I concede.

In my quest for what I
wanted,

here at last -
is what I need.

Unremembered

Were we ever
not together -
all this sense
of living passed?

Is this breath
a dream remembered -
our soul returned
for truth at last?

Is this our first
life everlasting -
was nothing here
when we began?
When we're safe
beyond this longing -
will we choose
to love again?

Will we wake
beyond this presence -
having knowledge
from the fall?
E'er we keep
this mortal promise -
and sleep the night
for touch recalled?

Is this time -
our only measure -
and moments shared,
our only need?

What of death
will find us wanting -
beyond this veil,
immortal seed.

Chaos

It's been so long
and yesterday
the blessing of today
was passed -
when all I feared
had come and gone,
and courage willed
me home at last.

No circumstance
to understand -
this futile fight -
these chains of time.
I will not raise my flag
to fall -
or give to love
by death defined.

For through my tears
a solace found -
and from these scars,
some comfort came.

Would wings decide
the storm's approach,
or those who love
be loved the same.

On other plains,
my worlds collide.
With pen in hand,
each page concedes
to write the rest
from here to there -
from now til then -
my place indeed.

So much of this
was left to chance -
in broken verse
my promise waits.
I wish somehow
I was there again -
when words resolved
to pen my fate.

Paradise Lost

The rivers
had grown colder -
seasons passed
when strangers came.
What was left
of ancient wisdom
in their hungry eyes
remained.

The sky -
no longer crimson
beneath a canopy of blue
Once ravens held the
corners -
now lies betrayed the
truth.

So few were left
to wonder - what of God
had kept them near
to the vision
of their fathers -
silent pleas
no one could hear.

The land
had all been bartered
a trade for freedom
what was lost...

In their haste
to find salvation
was paradise the cost?

Another place
a dream remembered -
time before the buffalo
came and went
the way of strangers -

leaving tears
no heart could hold.

Raindance

A solitude emptied
of all that was lacking -
was left there to warm
in the breath of the sun.

A place still forgiving
the ways we had
journeyed -
when truth come to find
us
the wanting undone.

Would time e'er replace
the feeling of wonder -
how sweet every measure
of tears from your soul.

A lifetime of waiting
what dreams were for
touching -
my heart reminiscing
the willing to hold.

An emptiness sits
as dew on the morning
pressed into places
my longing returns -

A dream without slumber
the night was so tender -
would the sin of
forgetting

this memory burn.

Tears fill my cup
to weaken my coffee -
the taste of forever
now mixed with the rain.

What sunrise is waiting
beyond this
remembrance -
would shine to the places
our love still remains.

Silver Lantern

Beneath a silver lantern
undaunted by the moon -
I wondered how we came to be
was it too late or soon...

Sometimes
an understanding -
were we too late to find
the message in the ways we came
to be this place in time...

Sometimes
there is no wonder -
for love will find me near
the place we dreamed
not far away
an evermore is here...

I cannot see
beyond this veil -
or will another life to come
another place
we find ourselves
the same as now -
as one

I am here

I am here
in the silence you know best
in the places you remember
far away with happiness

I am here
in the words you understand
a promise once was given
I would live to love again

I am here
in the essence of the night
in the flower's loving petal
in the dawn's restoring light

I am here
ever yours and still the same
as was written to forever
with the whisper
of my name

I am here
beyond the hurting
of goodbye
a hallelujah chorus
in the echo of a sigh

I am here
between the breaths
that hold you near
a moment not forsaken

I am love
- I am here

My Father's House

Around the bend
my Father lives -
and there with Him
my heart abides.

Beneath the climbing of
the rose -
His arms of love
are opened wide.

For He who waits
without remorse
and fills with love
my every need -
I come as one - a child
returned
as was my fate
to him relieved.

I cannot wait...
I shall not run...
for all my gifts were His
to me -
my breath, my soul,
my everything -
this day to live
eternally.

He knows me well
of all the rest.
His words of sweet
assurance come..

Beyond the dark -
a warm embrace
shall light the way
that leads to home.

Last Word

I'd give you the words
if I had them to offer
along with paper and ink
to impress -

I'd give you the sun
were darkness a
hindrance
your heart ever opened -
the need to confess.

I'd give you these walls
if you'd fill them with
moments
til none could remember
the day they were lost -
til none could remember
the silence of waiting
for what was worth
saying
no matter the cost.

I'd give you a rhyme
if was needed to guide
you -
a picture of heaven
I keep by the door -
my own empty pages
neglected and many -

I'd give you a sunset
a sunrise
and more.

I'd write you the lines
for living unspoken -
I know all the places
a muse can reside -
a shadow becoming
a silky white curtain -
moss to a memory
a heart to inscribe.....

I'd give you the silence
for I know in his
presence
many a word
has been known to
appear -

stuck between petals
dried and forgotten -
time becomes nothing
but ink into years.

I'd give you it all
if it meant you'd
remember
the warmth of the pen
your want to embrace.
If never another
word I was gifted -
I'd give you the last
my own to erase.

Essence of Smoke

Here in my heart
you'll always be -

Can't you see
you were there
all along...
not far from forgotten
but yet you remain -
a whisper of
yesterday's song.

Here in my soul
you'll always be -
a prayer to the gods
ever sweet...
a silent amen
for love that was blest -
a longing for time
to repeat.

Here in my eyes
you'll always be -
should the measure of
life
start to fade...
Here in my sight
the smile of hello -
dear as the moment
was made.

Here in my arms
you'll always be -
warmth to the skin
that you know...
Twilight dancing
in places we loved -
eternity spent long ago.

Here in my thoughts
you'll always be -
the promise
of one tender kiss...
coloring rainbows
the essence of smoke -
forever your name
on my lips.

Here in my heart
you'll always be -
Can't you see
you were there
all along...

Reminders of Me

I don't recognize
the words that are written -
they tell so much more
than the weight of the man.
Another I knew
was not so important -
but truth still becoming
what love understands.

Twice he was burned
his life fell to nothing -
still when he speaks
another I hear.
The hand that was pressed
to all that was sacred -
cut from the same
a moment so dear.

Now comes the man
and I've since forgotten
all I had promised
to remind him to be.
Would he ever remember
love without memory -
or do words
serve no purpose
but remind him of me.

Because...

you write
and beg the faithful fall
into the lair
your words designed
return the passion
and want for more
a world apart
you've given rhyme

you write
and for a moment spent
another bends
to hear your voice
another comes
across the way
would seem to them
the only choice

you write
and what of words are
left
you threw away
what wouldn't do
seemed no chore
but what of those
have not the words
were given you

you write
and books prepare to
grieve
forever still
their parchment page
a home for life
twas short but sweet
and measured not
by mortal age

you write
and words are ne'er the
same
though writ ten thousand
times before
you write
of all you've yet to find
and of the search
you write the more

you write
and legions rise as one
angels weep
for love you've failed
breath betrays a mossy
kiss
to seal the lips
her final tale

you write

Soldier

I was a soldier
held captive by a dream -
a story he had written
and mine alone to keep.
I would listen
til the candle barely
burned -
etched itself into my
memory
and I succumb to sleep.

I was a seeker
of every place he'd known
before -
every taste no longer
lingered
on the lips that told it
well.
I was wanting
of another place and time
-
where innocence was all
he knew
and I - a distant tale.

I am his memory -
how did he know we'd
come to this -
when all the songs his
memory wrote
were mine to write again.
I was a soldier
for every promise I had
made

now lingers like the
places
first were his -
remember when.

Let me tell you
of the boy you used to be
-
of the paths you used to
worry
and the lights you came
to see.
Let me whisper
til my tears have washed
your face -
and I alone remember
was your love -
my memory.

...let me tell you.

31

Arrow of Flowers

In His arms
He rocks you gently.
I see you there and I find peace -
for what of life
I cannot give you -
beyond this breath
a sweet release.

I cannot speak
without compassion
for other dreams you woke to see -
how could breath
be sworn to silence
or sorrow choose
this destiny.

May you know love
that needs no reason
that does not seek
its own to gain -
would that love be arms around you
until you find
your way again.

between the blades

I hear them pass
between the blades
where green the grass
once turned to red -
their essence wreathed
the giant oak -
would memory live
or time forget...

Their ancient ways
forsaken now -
a cardinal's stretch of
wings
to blue
ten thousand stars
their spirits burn -
how long their stay
this love to prove...

I hear a voice
becomes the wind
from yonder plains
their sorrows left -
where sons were died
and fathers fell -
a mother's pain
for winters wept...

Now to home
though distance far
and blossoms bloomed
too many years -

between the fall
and coming back
to find their truth
was welcomed here...

Beyond the green
a place remains -
smoke remembered
to the sun -
another dream
was theirs to live -
ere love returned
and life begun...

forgotten

Last night you were there
at the edge of my
memory -
and just for a moment
I'd forgotten your name.

I was leaving at sunrise
and you there remaining
- would ever tomorrow
be looked at the same.

So long had we traveled
a road never wanted
and stood by the death -
of dreams we once kept.

We stood for a moment
stars in the twilight -

shared more than one
sorrow
for living we wept.

There in my dream
you were bothered and
broken -
and I couldn't bear
the pain in your eyes.

I struggled with words
your name never spoken
-
convinced that my love
was a cruel disguise.

I woke with the dawn
the alarm never easy -
tears had been left
my pillow to wet -
but then with a smile
I knew you could hear
me -

as I spoke then the name
I shall never forget.

More Than This

I heard a voice
so low it came
a whisper almost
then a sigh -
I heard a bell
a feather floats
how long I heard
and wondered why.

So sweet repeating
over time
from year to year
the meaning missed -
became a truth
I longed to know

'you were meant
for more than this'...

I turned away
into the world
with stubborn will
I would not hear...
I closed my heart
to all but mine -
with no excuse
my purpose clear.

The calling swelled
and louder still
than times before
my soul remiss -
could I not see
the words were mine

'you were meant for more
than this'...

How long a course
of aging still -
do You not know
the plans I've made -
do You not know
the wrongs I've done -
how could You want
for love betrayed.

I hear You now
in every song
and on the wind
Your truth persists -
that I am more
than what I am

for I was meant
for more than this...

Missing Me

Before this day
another dawned -
but I can't recall the
scarlet hue -
or whether shadows fell
apart
or sprang to life
in morning dew.

I can't recall
what music played
the days I wandered
through the wood -
or nights I slept out on
the porch
a symphony
misunderstood.

I can't remember if I cried
when I saw that old man
bent to pray -
how long
I looked into his eyes
before I had to look away.

The flowers bloomed
last night and still -
I can't recall which star
was made -
or how the love
washed over me -
another blessing I
betrayed.

I saw a child out in the
field
just yesterday
a moments truth -
the winds of change
already blown
remembered in the lights
of youth.

A butterfly -
where silence stood
was melody once played
for me -
how many worlds for this
one came -
to find this piece of
destiny.

Let not my eyes
to beauty close -
or long for life another
place.
Let heaven find its home
in me -
and wonder fill my life
with grace.

Immortal Quest

Was not for glory
I was meant -
or for a kiss
my journey blessed.
Was not for law
my wrong resigned -
or martyrdom
to truth confessed.

Was not for barter
my refrain -
or words no one but I
could speak.
Was not for songs
another heard -
or for this life
my soul did seek.

Was not for death
my birth was come -
or shadows left
in living's stay.
Was not for dreams
another slept -
my want for wonder
gone astray.

Was not for
righteousness or right -
or miles to go
the worlds between.
Was not for love
though this enough -
immortal quest
for truth unseen.

Cast-a-ways

I looked into
the eyes of pain -
a raging kiln
of kindred blue -
into the hurt
another passed -

I saw into
the best of you.

I knew your fear.
I found the worst -
and warmed against
your shattered light.
For all you are
not one could boast -
a better place
or darker night.

When heroes pass
you wonder then
who left alive
will keep your flame -
who left behind
shall be your hope -
or mark the wall
that bears your name.

Tomorrow waits
a sacred few -
for what would come
your life deserves.
For love unmatched
by time or man -
shall find your home
by grace reserved.

Your longing
so familiar now
my words no different
than your own.
This path -
a gift of grace becomes
ere you would bear
these chains alone.

reverie

It is the sound
of ancient whispers
the sound of oceans
come to shore -
the hymn of truth
a pearly anthem -
a desperate plea
we gave before.

It is the voice
some angel singing
of other worlds
we've yet to see -
some lonely prayer
survived our season
recalls the best
is still to be.

It is the rush
of breath to living
the steady beat
of death's approach -
it is the promise
of salvation
becomes the now
for which we hope.

It is the silence
that remembers
every song of love
we sang -
it is the joy
we find in hearing
the ancient bell
that rings our name.

Evening Tide

Am I the wind
that pushed you to
surrender....
or ancient seas -
the blue where you
reside...
Another place -
a lighthouse
in the distance.

I brought you back
before the evening tide.

Am I the song
an echo still resounding -
a longing filled
with memories replayed.
Once was the voice
that brought the world
to silence -
I was the rain
that washed your need
away.

Am I the sun
or night forever longing -
a twilight sworn
your promises to keep.
Should love return
before this day is ended -
I'll be the dream
that wills your breath
to sleep.

beyond these days

Ten thousand words
and none to give you -
and yet I know
you know them all.
You have my heart
would breath remember
the ways we've come -
far from the fall.

Ere I would leave
the ways of winter
and find the spring
was where we loved.
Ere blossoms break
before this season -
another time
not soon enough.

The candle burns
forever changing -
and so it shall
beyond these days.
Shall light the place
for love's returning -
will find us here
another day.

40

Lily

The Easter lily
knows not of her grace -
or the essence
she spreads
to this dark lonely place.
She knows not the story
why she came
or would be.
Reminders of glory -
her own destiny.

She knows not the calling
or the crow
twice became -
or the ones that would
follow
and deny still His name.
She holds not the sorrow
to her heart
of that day -
what cries for remembrance
to the Father
were made.

She blooms
for this season
not for others regret -
for the promise
of mercy
a soul might forget.
She holds high
with purpose
a vision of then -
when a savior
was offered -
and born yet again.

cry from heaven

the thunder pounds
a bloody sky
where shadows hide
the sun's retreat
where treetops dance
against the wind
and blossoms bow
in reverence sweet

a silence wafts
before the boom
her fragile dawn
long since replaced
by echoes of forever more
the sky recalls
a moment's grace

tears of truth
and pounding rain
a cry so loud
the dead would wake
immortal truths
remain and still
was gift this son
our sin to take

a day as dark
this one and more
I can't deny
my destiny
between the wrong
the worthy rose
into the storm
was meant for me

take mine

Today my heart
is yours to keep -
yours to trust
ere your own would fail.
Should tears escape
the songs you sing -

my heart is yours
so wear it well.

Today my arms
will stretch to hold -
the loving gift
of who you are.
I know they'll reach
cross many miles -

a world away
not very far.

Today my smile
shall wear your name -
to fill the hurt
you bear alone.
Til light shall come
to warm your face -

always - my heart
shall be your home.

Today and then
ten thousand more -
for all your days
this one shall beat.
The song you know
we sing so well -

ere echoes sound
and love repeat.

just to see her smile

if this is ours
a loving land
when will we learn
the power of man
what was the choice
became the dream
when all that's left
is days between

when we were young
we had it all
did we look to now
and see the fall
did we hold the rose
and touch her skin
before our choice
remember when

were we too wise
not young enough
to see the wonder
was ours to love
when life was worth
the choices made
we held her close
but still for trade

comes now the time
we surely see
how less our love
has proved to be
we threw her down
and took her truth
filled her lungs
with prideful youth

filled her streams
with oil and gas
her crystal blue
was gone at last
we showed our love
a selfish rite
would burn her sun
into the night

into the rose
her fragile fade
her petals lost
one last parade
the cricket's song
to memory lies
now plays to life
of our demise

her trust of us
her loving will
all we could love
and love us still
would she return
forgiving this
for what we gave
a bitter kiss

we have a choice
to live again
to clear the air
where love has been
to blue the seas
ere life return
to see her smile
for lessons learned

unremembering

I wish I had held
to moments more dearly -
to songs that were played
on the breath of a sigh.
I wish I had watched
as wonder unraveled
and slept when it ended -
a lifetime passed by.

I wish I had prayed
and waited the blessings
as sure in their coming
my delight when they
came.
I wish I had slept
long past your leaving -
and woke to a morning
where love still remained.

I wish I had loved
when the words
were still tender -
their silence remembered
a place long ago.
I wish I had listened -
did you whisper forever
in rhyme before reason -
and wanting to know.

I wish I had gone
when the going was easy

the reasons to linger
not much to confess.

A road that was fated -
the way back
forgotten.
My chance for
redemption
not bartered for less.

I wish I had dreamed
the real of what mattered
- were moments
pretending
just time passing
through.
I wish I had held
a little while longer -
ere time steal the
memory of wishing
for you.

And then

Once I sailed
beyond these stars
and floated there in
precious haze -
I learned to breathe
beyond the dark
and danced within
the moon's embrace.

I touched the face of God
and then -
pretended life would be
enough.
A canyon filled
with nevermore -
could never comprehend
my love.

I marked the skies
with scattered prose -
lines collected from my
youth.
Memories now come and
gone -
are poor reminders
of the truth.
Was work in vain
light to behold -
the journey long
this dream to claim.

Was evermore a place too
far -
its destiny
forever changed.

I still recall
that place beyond -
was wreathed by worlds
another dreamed.
Became the stars
that light my sky -
a path of rainbows
laid between.

How little we
of wonder know -
a pebble tossed
into the sea -
where universes
rise and fall -
within the breath
you give to me.

making sense

from me to you
(and back again)
no more a breath
(though leagues may be)
would grace decide
between the two
and make (of each)
one less (than we)

within this realm
where angels watch
as petals rush
(to greet the sky)
where mountains climb
above (the seas)
to watch the sailor's sails
(go by)

where seasons pass
(and melt to dust)
was but for love
(this light began)
for every blade of grass
(was bent)
someday will rise
to green (again)

what gentle winds
shall fell our gods
and push (for reason)
truth enough
when what becomes
(we understand)
in this immortal gift
(of love)

barefoot girls

You are there
and I don't have
the words to spend -
I would give
of every treasure
just to hear your voice
again.

Your heart -
will it beat
again with mine...
would your laughter
fill the heavens
but for me
just one more time.

I would plead -
sell my soul
for nothing less
than the promise
of forever -
given this
your place to rest.

Let me be -
I won't die
for pride or shame...
but for you
amounts to nothing -
take my breath
as yours to claim.

In the shallows
precious souls
one light become -
barefoot girls
will wade the river -
loving arms
will guide
us home.

with the apostles

I've been known
to seek religion
in the backseat of a
Buick -
to find my home
in lonely nights
turned blue by love's
regret.
I've toasted life
with dime store wine
and knelt with the
apostles -
sang Jesus Loves
til I was drunk
on bartered dreams
and bets.

I wanted more
and took the chance -
gambled with my share
of loss.
I took a spin
on fate's long haul
and willed the rest away.
I've burnt my knees
on sacred men -
and damned their will
in leaving.
Whispered hymns
against the dark
that melted sin
to day.

Too many times
and then once more -
was bruised and for
another wept.
Ashes into laundromats
and longing spilled to
verse.
Poems filled with
evermore -
a candle barely flickers
to hide the smile
I wear for you -

there lies the truth
I curse.

empty rooms

there's a place
called lonely
just this side of giving in
miles between
this life and living
twilight glows
where love has been

there's a place
called sadness
where lovers go
when love is gone
lots of room
reserved for silence
longing nights
now spent alone

there's a place
called wanting
simple songs
no hand can play
empty rooms
an echo slumbers
beyond this night
another day

there's a place
called leaving
not far enough
I've heard them tell
hangs a sign
outside forever
good intentions -
the road to hell

there's a place

called ever
I stayed there once
was long enough
time to dream
beyond tomorrow
where lonely lives
but never loves

storm clouds

just yesterday
these lines were lost
then everything I loved
returned
moss betrayed
to ruby lips
and seeds but for their
blossom
yearned

I found the page
one righteous fault
was smeared with doubt
before we knew
and laughter swelled
as red balloons
and floated far
beyond my view

a wind of words
and random thought
turned my
simple world around
a song I sang
ten thousand years
was played for me -
how still
the sound

gilded edges
and bottled ink
a want for life
now stirs again
when all was lost
has come to home
a storm embraced
by love
begins

51

Love Already There

Was there a moment
I heard you singing -
and felt your touch
upon my skin.
A faded memory
beyond the mirror -
you came so near
to life again.

I saw a petal
pale and perfect -
seeds of hope
spilled on the grass.
I saw a wing
left on the meadow -
for what of truth
was meant to last.

These your clothes
still bear
your presence -
perfume plays
on sheets you wore.
Morning breaks -
fulfilled the promise
that time would pass
to evermore.

Forever here
your love will linger -
in silence sweet
I'll call your name.
Assured of heaven -
a grand reunion
where we shall live
and love the same.

a week ago

A week ago
last Saturday -
I learned (at last) to fly.
I raised my arms
into the wind -
and sailed
beyond the sky.

I steered against
an Easter chill -
heard whispers soft
above the roar.
Banked along
a canyon's crest -
between her jasper
shores.

With folded wing
I split the blue -
and fell ten thousand
leagues for death.
Closed my eyes
against the wave -
and willed my battered
soul
to breath.

Quiet now.....
a ruffled flirt -
steady beats my
wing-ed heart.
Ethers filled
with silent song -
a place I loved
now worlds apart.

A week ago
last Saturday -

I learned (at last)
to fly

53

moments passed

Were you always there
a dream away -
hiding
in a shadow's face?
How could you know
the miles we came -
to bloom the rose
for friendship's sake?

Before you were
my purpose lost...
I think I heard your
name
somewhere.....
I'm sure the path
was marked for you...
before you came
my way to share.

What time is left
or vows to keep
lifetimes passed - this
one to prove
this place of light
was ours to be -
one half of love
the whole of truth.

Is that your voice
above the fray -
a highway left
for streets of gold...
ribbons weaved
of moments passed -
returned as this
your heart to hold.

Did e'er you know
before as now
a multitude of blessings
fair-
for lives returned
this one to find -
or joys so sweet
that none compares...

Were you always there
a dream away –

Before You Were Gone

I knew of surrender
long before you were gone -
a fall from hereafter
to where we belong.
I knew of your laughter
before I could hear -
a song
unremembered -
was still just as clear.

I knew of this moment
though how
I'm not sure -
before I had journeyed
this path to endure.
I questioned the reasons
not enough
for to stay -
but for this - life eternal
wakes within
a new day.

I knew of the sorrow
but loved all I could -
what for more
I might bargain...
Another dream understood.
I knew
but could not answer
longing burned
sweet enough -
one voice on the ethers
ripples still
of your love.

left for me

before I found
these sacred words
were meant for me
and writ in red
before I walked
a path of grace
I walked the way
of fire instead

before my knees
were bruised in prayer
and silence stirred
against my truth
I found my hope
in sinful men
and waited love
to offer proof

before I cried
and woke alone
before I gave
...and gave
......and gave
I heard the voice
above the night
but for my soul
another saved

before this night
of sweet refrain
pages worn
by tears and time
I found the place

my story told
before my breath
this one to find

before this day
another set
on memories
I made with blood
before this light
became my own
I walked the waves
became
the flood

before I loved
I loved the world
not one the less
or one the more
I cried for those
who cursed my name
between the words
I spoke before

how long the page
where promise slept
restored from death
anew to be
the evermore
I came to find
was writ in red
and left
for me

56

reminisce-

I wish I had known
what was mine
yesterday -
would we live in
forever -
'ere time fall
away.

I wish I had seen
past the truth
of your eyes -
your soul
crossing over -
filled with wondrous
surprise.

I wish I had known
the blossoms
would bloom -
that death
held no ransom
to love's sweet perfume.

I wish I had been -
stronger still -
I am now.
That I had loved you
more dearly -
than time
would allow.

I wish I had held
with but one
final kiss -

I had sealed
your remember
to moments as this.

I wish I had dreamed
and never woke
from our love -
would fate be
forgotten -
was wishing
enough.

before there was me

there's so much to say
and less worth repeating
a lifetime of waiting
this moment to come
I think I should write
but words
have no meaning
when compared with this
moment
and promise undone

there's so much to know
and too much
to measure
days become nothing
surrendered to time
changes forgotten
names seldom mentioned
the truth but a memory
of me left behind

long I have lived
and lost through so
many
another - one day
fades the chill
of before
death into dreams
a song on the ethers
turned from the veil
to whispers
once more

what good is goodbye
if never is lessened
by the pull of forever
and love still to be
seeds fell to blossom
their perfume remembers
what withered one winter
before there was me

Returned From the Fall

Would 'ere I be more
than a dream could recall
a voice from the darkness
returned from the fall.
Would 'ere I be love
but much more
than we shared -

ten thousand years
passing -
one night
unprepared.

Would 'ere I be more
than a touch
you once knew -
or perfume that wreaths
a longing or two.
Would 'ere I be loved
even now -- all this time -
a memory forsaken
to reason resigned.

Would 'ere I be this
and no more than a tear
for angels now watching
or saints ever dear.
Would words be
remorseful -
lines penned to the grave.

Much more than eternal -
this moment
could save.

Would 'ere I be more -
less than love
so divine -
unburdened by living
these shackles of time.
Would 'ere I be waiting -
nearer still
than your breath -
The place we are - always

- keeps no memory
of death.

for the taking

If all that I wanted
was mine for the taking -
and prayer - but a
process -
I had to go through -
I'd spend every night
alone with my pleading -
hands held to heaven

what more could I do?

If all that I dreamed
was waiting the twilight -
a pillow so soft
once cradled my head.
I'd slip through the sun
to run in the shadows -
would suffer the stars -
might burn
to my bed.

If all that I loved
were offered
this moment -
no sweeter my words
one song could repeat.
I'd bathe in the light
of candles and courage -
walk through the flame
with love on my feet.

If all that I was -
this mortal companion -
flesh come to be
from a dream - long ago.
I'd whisper your name
as once it was spoken -
revealed every truth
you were destined
to know.

If all that I give
is the wisdom to wonder

- answers to questions
still longing for voice.
I'd be - one more time -
the best you remember -
a time not forgotten -
a dream turned
to choice.

one more yesterday

Whenever I'm restless
I think of October -
golden red leaves
made crisp by the sun.
I think of a silence -
so pure
it was ringing
a wind through the trees
-
eternity come.

I think of my words -
and others
unspoken -
whispered transgressions
warmed sweet
to goodbye.
Long lazy mornings
of no longer waiting -
what fate might
remember -
the chill of July.

I remember those days -
even now
they are treasured -
wing-ed white truth
set free on the night.
Promises left
in pieces of summer -
a glimmer
of something -
we willed
into life.

I've known other times
the years - ever tender
given to dreams -
just a moment away.
Beneath a red sky
of swirling
October -
I waited forever -
one more
yesterday.

what more

Beyond the edge
of turning back -
I stand as one - not
passed before.
I stand as life
unlived 'til now

outside this world -
another door.

Were lips
once sealed -
before the night
when wisdom came
a road unmarked -
by nevermore and
ancient ways

beyond the grave -
beyond the dark.

No words survived -
no parchment bed
would speak of love
a moment missed -
Would be the song
that wore your name
when evermore -
returned as this.

I've given all -
you cannot know
how dear the gift was my
embrace.
Beyond the love
that keeps not time -

I come to thee
this sacred place.

Would longing fail
or mountains mourn
for granite saints -
an sleepless dream.
Would angels
kneel before the king -
and choose
no more -
these mortal streams.

From death
to life -
how great the fall
was fate to write our
memory.
What more of love
we've yet to find -

beyond this veil
of destiny.

this day

But for this
we were waiting -
for this day -
above them all.
This reason for believing
-
promise lingered
from the fall.
This day
oh so glorious -
none before
or since compare
to the sun
through the maples -
scent of longing
fills the air.

I woke
slow from dreaming -
wondrous fog
wreathed my mind.
Orchids bloomed
from the ashes
another place -
love defined.
None so fair - none so
fleeting
as this breath
a sweet release...
into the light
we were going
beyond this day
of destinies.

From this day
one more repeating
would we then choose
the more to love -
would we replace
our everafter -
with moments here
or remnants of.
I've been there
and I bear witness -
to what awaits
our will to be.
Beyond the stars
a twinkle glimmers
of what is ours -
eternity.

roses and rust

there are pages
unwritten
to time and distrust
markers were left
of roses and rust
I knew you were leaving
long before you were
gone
a dark lonely road
leading home

there are secrets
unspoken
we choose to believe
how sweet their
remembrance
one breath to conceive
ten thousand lifetimes
for one would I live
in trade for the past
I forgive

there are echoes
and always
a home we know best
people we loved -
a dream unconfessed
no turning back easy
no rewind
on the day -
just this - the now
we betray

I can't say I blame you
I won't say goodbye
some things have no
reason
but won't be denied
are words without
memory
the reasons they came
as fleeting -
the sound
of my name

the rites of sin

spread
your eager fingers
master
give to me
the rites of sin
make a place
ere I shall tarry
to dream
this night
with you again

beneath the green
was born of envy
fragile lines
of solace write
across the page
a bloom
remembers
where once was dark
became the light

let us wake
to everafter
a sweet embrace
we live to tell
souvenirs
forgotten - never
tangled vines
from truth
availed

spread
your eager fingers
master
give to me
the rites of sin

given to angels

I am the echo -
of whispered
tomorrows
- a flutter-by feeling
made real
by the wind.
I am the touch
so close
and so distant
a longing for something -
the place
we begin.

I am the name
you won't speak aloud -
a one time
remembered -
three words unprofessed.
I am the truth
you willed into being -
became of creation
the wonder
of 'yes'.

I am the silence
that stirs in the darkness
- long winter drives
on roads
far from home.
I am the snow
that melts to your
windshield-
warms to your love
in moments alone.

I am the music
was given to angels -
left on your door
the day
we first met.
Places you loved -
no less
in remembrance -
richer for time
- no room
for regret.

I am the promise -
won't be forsaken
 - written to skin
ten thousand lives past.
Clings to your fate
with sweet
everafter -
awaits our forever -
surrender
at last.

a place to dwell

Within the dark
where silence reigns -
I hear my breath
so still
she creeps.
A trembled heart
at work with word -
would promise
choose this vow
to keep.

Beyond the verse
in living passed -
I wonder -
will they understand...
How much the tale
was theirs to own -
my only gift
these willing hands.

Beyond the dark
another light...
Of loneliness -
I know him well.
Adrift in words
were meant
for none -
but found in me
a place
to dwell.

Until Then

I see you there.....
in dreams
we were making.
You're sitting in shadows
- and don't know
I'm here.....
A long lonely way -
seven sands
still I wander...
back to this moment
remains
just as dear.

I've waited ten thousand
lives
to remember -
the road back to you
was always the same.
Counted by stars
that burned
into nothing....
a candlelight circled
as dust into flame.

I know
that you're lonely.
I've been
only sleeping...
not far from your bed -
the warmth of your sighs.
Tomorrow shall come -
no more
will you worry....

What loss has you
grieving -
for death's brief
goodbyes.

Still in your tears
I count every season...
a touch
once so fleeting...
Will we find it
again....
Would love be forever -
so soon
I shall hold you...

Alone in
this silence -
I wait until then.

ruby red

her hair was spun
by gypsy moths
and weaved with ribbons
ruby red
her eyes
a shade of cappucine
gave life to every
dream or dread

she spoke in words
not one could know
a language
only she could speak
a universe
where all was love -
would curse the sailor's
longing - weak

her fragile hands
a raven's wing
fluttered soft the beat
of care
a blossomed white
gardenia sweet
was her perfume
a lover's fare

she breathed
ten thousand years
of light
and knew of things
most men could not
she harbored tears
for what was spent
and spoke with kind
of love
forgot

what time was hers
no one could say
another birth
from sorrows cost
what kiss was made
to give away

what ruby red
a gypsy moth

what man

What man would know
the face of God -
or wear it well
for those who love.
What warrior
came against the paint -
this life to live -
this good enough.

What man of all -
I cannot say
what name was his
a dreamer's dream...
What comfort
now could ever match
the pain of loss -
the days between.

What man is this
we loved him so -
through words -
a world - we came to be.
His heart of truth
was not for us -
but gave to life
a light
to see.

When I am old
(I'm not so far) -
and worn by time
the next to meet.
I'll think of him
my brother strong -
and wait the day
again we meet.

last time

The last time
I held you -
the train was just
leaving.
A pink piece
of twilight
was burned
soft as coal.
A whistle of promise -
came sweet
down the canyon -
for a moment
forever
was a hand
we could hold.

The last time
I saw you -
was just around
morning.
We rolled into Beaumont
and stopped for a bite...
I remember that look -
how distant
and dreamy -
reflecting on something
we'd lost
to the light.

The last time
I kissed you -
was two o'clock Sunday...
bent over journals -
some place
never been.
A dark stretch of highway
and no place
for turning -
back to beginning
we wandered
again.

The last time
I called you -
I suffered my longing
how deep the missing -
a place
you once knew.
How dear
the memory
of roads left to travel -
ere time give me
mercy -

another
last time
with you.

play me

Wander
with me
down the ancient path...
into the meadow's
deepened dark...
petals torn and faded
pink.
Come with me--
play me --
your music --
a laughter shared
a moment
undeserved --

not one
would know.....

Words sail
beyond the trees.
Silence wears
a winter dress --
A sweeter kiss
I could not give
or take mine own
from passion's lips.

With green leaves
we paint the boughs....
anew at last
the place
we loved.

The breeze bears
every dream....
a silver sun burns.
In her light
I find your smile.
Lifetimes between,
mine is the open hand
that bids you come...

And the universe
cries --
I will.

shadows of a dream

For this I waited --
never frightened
by your touch.
For all that you were
needing --
I wanted way too much.
I loved you for the
reasons
you could never
understand...

the universe you gave to
me --
a love without demand.

Beyond the twilight --
shadows gathered
from the past
-- moments never left
behind
but never meant
to last.
A jealous moon
once listened in
on words we left
unspoken.
No room for talk
of what might be --
or promise yet
unbroken.

For this I waited --
ten thousand more
I would.
What light was
never meant for light --
is seldom
understood.

Whatever is
will always be --
and nonetheless
for time between.
What evermore
was left that day --
in shadows
of a dream.

the place I remember

was your promise
a face in the crowd
(someday) - a destiny true
a voice on the wind
reminds me (again)
the place (I remember)
as you

was our moment
(no more than) a dream
a kiss at the gate --
letting go
we lingered that day
(yet time gave away)
to truths
we were destined
to know

was our purpose
a blessing (to touch)
faded - a photograph (now)
a strange black (and white)
conceded to light
and more than this world
would allow

was your whisper
the song (I would hear) --
an echo of longing (out loud)
is yesterday gone
(or still holding on)
still waiting
your face (in a crowd)

woodsmoke and cinder

Returning
long after the weeds
had grown over...
The gate swinging open
was left not for me.
Would love
be reminded
the ways --
I had traveled
for this was I longing --
immortal to be.

The promise
of time --
lays sweet on the meadow --
hushed by a moment
of sunrise to breath...
The cannon's refrain
of lingering sadness --
fell to that morning
a whisper
of death...

Returning
long after the weeds
had grown over...
a place on the pasture
remembers us well...
Was evermore wasted
on woodsmoke
and cinder --
what secrets surrendered
were never meant
to tell...

without a sound

When will the brighter
star
be wished...
and somewhere far
be given light...
Would then the universe
return --
for such as this --
a perfect night.

A walk beyond
the meadow green --
bathed in shadows
cast the moon.
Heaven's choir -- now
fell to earth...
the smell of hay --
a cricket's croon.

Alone with this
my first true love --
warm the chill
becomes my shawl.
Stilled -- the essence
of my breath.
Her language -- mine --
the spirit's call.

Bare feet dance
on polished stone --
the path of angels
left for me...
Around the barn
and down the hill --
a river plays
sweet melody.

I close my eyes
a stolen kiss --
memories glide
between the trees.
Tender fingers brush my
skin --
my name -- a whisper --
rides the breeze.

Canopies of Venus --
Mars --
wait for words
where none are found...
Was love --
the altar I was knelt
and life -- the song
without a sound.

the weight of waiting

I've seen that smile
I know the wearer --
tender hides the scars
inside.
Time for changing --
not much longer.

Days to evermore --
we ride.

I see you standing
past the pavement...
black the cherries --
still you bleed.
What of manna rained
from heaven --

would your love
at last be freed...

I know regret
a time remembered --
guilty works to feel the
same...
was the touch
that left you longing --

became the kiss
that wears your name.

Would truth be lost
to moments waiting --
Eternity --
shall pass unseen...
Where was love
is still -- and present --

shall be no less
for days between.

A fleeting smile
I know the reasons --
were not for words
and destiny.
Silence bears the weight
of waiting --

for what of love
is still to be...

deliberate pause

Walking beneath stars at dusk,
doves coo (quietly) to one another,
songs only they (of dove wisdom) can understand...

and I wonder at their (selfless) lament...
What (can they whisper that) I do not know?

What invisible mysteries
do the waves instill -- crashing against the cliffs....
(who can tell me)
what secrets the rain confesses to the violet dawn,
is its suffering (made) lesser
by the crimson sunset?
Is there a place (we've yet to find)
that waits under evergreen canopies of silence...
attuned to (the cry of) rainbows...
or is that for the poet (alone) to know....

Ten thousand paper birds
(without the heritage to) become feathers...
but still they drift...tangled not (by expectations)
no tears for tiny fingers
(that pried) their inanimate bones...
they've yet to understand
they cannot soar...
and (so) they do...

Can the only secret (worth discovery) be
that a simple morning song...
bellowed atop (a twist of) cooper line
is more (precious) than a symphony of perfectly managed
notes...

and that love needs no reason (to be)
(undone by questions -- why not)
beyond a moment's (deliberate) pause.....

the engineer

Was fate
the way the train
rolled in --
a whistle stop
before the stall --
Was just a place --
was 'meant to be' --
one last long breath
before the fall.

Were rails
between the sycamores,
a black hawk soared
above the pines.
I heard you ask
as I turned
to leave --

'will I see you there'

how sweet --
those lines...

Was slow
the rasp of my reply --
a moment late
you'd turned
away...

Wheels were
grinding steel to smoke...

were you ever there --
(I dare not say).

Was long
the wait for reason
come...
I've stalked
the darkness -- stilled for
light.
Sometimes I swear
the silence screams --
sometimes a whistle
haunts the night...

Was fate
the way the train
rolled in --
a whistle stop
before the stall --

79

winter socks

look at me
what remains of love's
design....
morning splashed
mascara bleeds
in passions left
behind

look at me
dressed in winter socks
and lace
silver strands
a locket wove --
from souvenirs
displaced

look at me
do these eyes
a future tell
was yesterday
a price too much --

this looking back
-- our hell

look at me
for a while --
let sorrows come
between the
past was yours --
now mine --
were days denied
by none

look at me
when ivy
steals your kiss
when orchids bloom
a purple sky
will we find time
for this

look at me --
destiny -- we proved
again
mornings passed
into the sun

shall light
my nights 'til then...

look at me...

80

I wish you knew

was a morning stilled
by dew to frost
steam rolled off a winter lawn
was there before
the sun woke up
I lay beneath the stars
at dawn

I listened hard
would comfort come
eyes closed tight,
my arms spread wide...
would I be blessed
to hold you still --
I spoke your name
and wept inside

I wish you knew
of thoughts unshared --
of love unspoken
my sore regret
for moments passed
alone and far,
what might have been --

will you find me
yet

a startled bird
a swirling leaf
a gentle sigh -- as breath to skin

I sense you here
as warmth -- the sun
is woke from sleep
to burn again

blacktop truth

Before you found
your way to me --
did you journey long
a blacktop truth.
Did you breathe the
smoke
of chain and steel --
Did you read the stars,
and pray
for proof...

Before I found
my way to you --
from moon to moon,
I traveled far.
I strained to hear
the engine's drone --
might lead me back
to where
we are...

Before your head
was brushed my breast --
what pillow
claimed your fondest
dream...
Was this -- the place
imagined then --
or faith more real
than life
would seem.

Before my head
had found its place
in arms -- what fate --

might keep me there.
Was not a dream
I'd held before --
would know
this heaven
anywhere...

Before you spoke
poetic verse --
were other words
your choice for fame...
When came the first
emotion wrote --
was not for touch
you loved
became.

Before I spoke
were notes to calm --
a whispered plea
to write again.
I held your words
against my soul --
e'er love resolve
my search
to end...

Before these trials
a distance made --
and silence stretched
from me
to you --
Was this the way
we came before --
Was evermore --
a place we knew..

82

spinning

I dreamed of
kings and kingdoms,
Camelot and merlin --
legend forged by magic
and desire.
I dreamed of knights
approaching --
might find this maiden
waiting --
for all this everafter
might inspire.

I dreamed of pearls
and whiskey --
a lazy Sunday morning,
news from home --
across and down
the same.
I dreamed of
picket fences,
a porch to wrap around
us --
closing time, and
calling stars by name.

I dreamed of distant
highways, were made for
this horizon...
a destination yet to be
revealed.
I dreamed of clay
and coyotes,
a hand that fit me
walking...
miles ahead to wonder
how I feel.

I dreamed of boots
and perfume,
a light across the
meadow --
drawers were filled
with treasures
I loved best.
I dreamed of
Sunday mornings,
a winding road to take
me,
back to the arms --
where dreaming
I shall rest.

on fire

Was once a spark,
a tiny flame --
a breath of truth
I knew could spread --
would give to others
light and love --

might catch the world
on fire instead...

Was gave to one
and then again --
as soon the flames
rose all about...
A Circle burned
of loving hearts --
was gift to shadows
dark with doubt...

Was once a song
I whispered low --
but now their voices
rise with mine...
Their open arms
what proof I need -

was once a spark
of love divine.

driving blind

Was used to be
that I would sail,
with all the universe
to win --
rising tall
above the seat --
a flag unfurled
into the wind.

Would spend
my days with arms
outstretched --
my hair, a raven swirl of
youth.
I'd hear the
folded cards spin round -
-
their melodies of
fated truth.

I'd climb the hills,
with push so hard --
each breath,
as if my last to give...
When then I came
upon the crest --
my treasure sure,
this joy to live.

Beneath the sun,
a slant of girl --
with tangled limbs
and distant dreams --
would race
the wind behind
closed lids --
a destiny
of worlds unseen.

resurrection

the snow (the past)
had washed away --
blossom crushed
beneath the spread
seeds (were promise)
never lost
awaiting now --
to be (instead)

the first of green,
a burst of red,
violets pressed
to (patient) bloom --
remembered
essence stirred to life --
the dead (re)born
to sweet perfume

a needle (stiff)
from winter nights --
his fate to stand
in sacrifice
has waited (hard)
this time of warmth
might bring his
(aching) arms
to life

a shadow fell
but (never) knew
to count the days
might pass (til then)
without the sun's
undying love --
the bud would break
(and truth would end)

honeysuckle
weights the vine
where (yesterday)
her secrets kept
a schedule made
of birth and death --
promise (blooms)
where promise slept

evermore to write

I do not want
a copper bed,
but a bit of cedar, lined with patch...
songs I sang
when no one heard,
of a place I (lonely) knew...

I want a pen and paper,
just enough...
a lantern,
and a crust of bread...

Let them carry me
at twilight...
barefoot to the meadow...

...to sleep beneath
a crescent moon, shadowed
by my fathers...

a serenade of drums and rifles,
oleander and lilac...

I want a story barely started...
and evermore to write...

tiger lily

How long the ways
to get here --
past the search
to understand...
Was never less
than who I am --
no half to give
my hand

-- was waiting not
another piece
would make me
more of me,
Or make me less
than I am now --
a spirit -- whole
and free

When in my eyes,
I see myself...
a hand that fits
the same as mine
I breathe --
another world becomes,
was not by this
defined

When heard a voice
I whispered --
read aloud
these words again...
Memory traced
the path of love --
was light
where light
began...

Were one before;
will one remain --
What fate could separate
the whole...
for what is more
than love -- than I
the same to be
-- one soul

teacher of fishermen

let me be
as you have dreamed
as first you saw
when in my hands
you placed another
seeking love...
you gave me heart
to understand...

let me be
as you have seen
with eyes that see
before and still...
the roads I've walked
ahead to clear
my destiny
shall be your will...

let me be
as you have proved
a light to burn
into the black...
let me be
the candle's glow
across the dark
would bring
them back

let me be
as you have need
guide my thoughts
as day begins
let me be the truth
made real...
would teach to fish
the souls of men

everyone (but me)

Was understood
by everyone --
(everyone but me).
How could I walk
beside the fence,
with sorrow (for the
tree)...
Was understood
how much was gained
but none (had kept) the
loss --
would glorify the
damage done,
to reconcile the cost...

Was understood
the flowers
could not bloom
without some plan...
that vines
might grow (too freely)...
and weeds devour
the land...

Was understood
the earth could not
survive
(without) our care...
What highways
might we sacrifice,
to grow
a meadow there...
If walls were fell,
and in their stead
a forest had returned...

what heavens could be
witnessed...
with just these lights
to burn...

Was understood
that truth might bring
some wonder
we had missed...
might fill our lives
with purpose,
give us reason
(to exist...)
Would take the place
of churches,
synagogues of glass (and
steel)...
A blanket spread
beneath the stars,
the best of us -
fulfilled...

Was understood
that some would scoff
while others
did without...
Was chose the way
to wisdom...
suffered times
of fear and doubt...
Was understood
(but never spoke)
how far our minds
might reach...
when gave to truth

90

(was meant for truth...)
and never meant
to preach

Was understood
tomorrow would not change
the ways we've come...
for only this
(the now we make)
shall claim the battle won...

A world exists
beyond today --
(remembrance of a tree)

was understood
by everyone --
everyone but me...

hush

I can't recall the words
last spoke...
guess we didn't know it then
there'd come a time
we'd wonder back...
o'er places might have been...
We'd ask the same
hard questions...
sit in silence framed by light,
whisper promise (never more)
the last we said
goodnight...

I can't recall the words
last spoke...
least of all, the letting go...
was never thought the last
would last...
I'd take them back I know....
would live in moments
sad (and sweet) --
silence without care --
hands to hold (remembered)...
Leaves were falling
everywhere...

I can't recall the words
last spoke...
I turned and you were gone,
had evermore
returned as fate...
the love I'd waited on...
Was frozen by the stillness --
whirling reds and
autumn gold...

A growing chill (I should have felt)
the winter on my soul...

I can't recall the words
last spoke...
but I close my eyes
sometimes...
and hear your tender
'come to me'...
in words (the weight of wine...)
I speak your name
into the dark,
I wonder - do you hear,
words I kept from last we spoke...
their melody so clear...

I can't recall the words
last spoke...
might have known
their warmth I'd miss..
What destiny still lingers
in the message
of a kiss...
What more to say
when time will come...
than moments (shall) recall,
What words were left
unspoken...

-- I miss them most of all...

chameleon

Was first
the painted frogs that came
from underneath the boughs...
had found a door -
forgot to lock -
I think about them now.
Was worried they
had wandered blind
when cast into the sun -
Was first, and then
he followed her -
I wondered what I'd done...

Was next
the flame of blue and gold,
heartbeats thumped
beneath their skin -
were chased along
the window's edge -
would fate decide (to let them in)...
Shadows stirred their
hiding place...
changing colors (just for fun)...
Was first, and then
he followed her -
I wondered what I'd done...

Was June
and all the creeks had dried
the river's edge - a mile away.
Asphalt buckled by
the heat, living streams
succumb to clay...
Slow, they scraped
while traffic buzzed...
stopped to watch (the only one)...

Was first, and then
he followed her -
I wondered what I'd done...

Was years
and then I found them,
making love beneath
the eaves...
Tangled up in silken knots
nestled in the leaves.
Black as bits of raven storm,
their majesty begun...
Was first, and then
he followed her -
I wondered what I'd done...

Was cool
the morning's southern sky...
baked the rocks
on which we slept...
apart, together
all the same -
were memories (survived) I kept.
Immortal spirit,
freed again --
eternity waits for none...

Was first, and then
he followed me -
I wondered what I'd done...

what we don't....

Stillness speaks in words
I seldom hear...
candles burn - scented yesterday.
The sweetest night was past...
from places dear
another time - a place I might have stayed...
But silence knows the song I sing...
dancing barefoot in the dark,
waltzing past the moon while others doze -
closer to forever than the stars...

Was once confessed but met
with disbelief;
we've forgotten what it means to dream
caught in papers - there the evening news;
everything (and nothing) as it seems...
But I've discovered
hope in discontent,
moments found me lucid (eyelids closed)...
simple prayers I never spoke aloud
are whispered soft -
communion, no one knows...

from silver wings that flicker on the
lawn...
past the purple glow of Al Jabba,
I've met ten thousand more
that have no names...
history betrayed their moment's mark...
But for the dreamer,
once had walked alone
another shining moment we forgot...
caught in memory
and written there...
time may have forsaken,
but we have not...

Between the ticks of ten and two,
all I am is come for me...
Twilight pulls the mortal world to bed,
and I pretend to let
the veil of slumber fall around...
were only I so willing to
be led...
Would pass between the shadows
cast by misery and want...
would rest and wake tomorrow --
nothing strange.
Complacency is petals wept
before the blackest swan;
hands are stopped -
eternity is changed...

And there, across the table
a familiar face,
eyes are met with knowledge
of the truth...
Presence finds assurance
in the noonday sun...
Coincidence, a world denied the proof...
A fleeting smile, a knowing laugh,
secrets shared by strangers...
candles burn - scented yesterday.
The sweetest night was past...
from places dear
another time - a place I might have stayed...

silence knows the song I sing...
dancing barefoot in the dark,
waltzing past the moon while others doze,
closer to forever than the stars...

closer to forever
than the stars...

gathered in me

Was not the first
I'd come again...
reeking of woodsmoke
folded near inside my
shirt...
names that should be
new;
the taste of somewhere
else
triggered in the calling.
Silence (clinging) feels the
same
a sweet familiar love -
remembered all the
reasons why I left...
to come again
pulling at pieces
truth exposed -
another piece of cloth,
clothes that fit me (still...)
I've walked the house
once we built -
shaded by the orchard --
Planted small,
and grew into the barn...
Now both
are gone, and I (unaware)
possess the only picture
of how it was...
the broken yard and
crooked gate,
cattle nursed by a patch
of weed (and will...)
a swing of mismatched
boards...slouched below
outstretched arms

an oak --
your father planted
(your mother cursed)...
Was there we loved...
(as no one ever had),
feather mattress
stuffed and stitched
(new)
for us, and wrapped
in sacks of blue...

We spoke in hushed
whispers
(secrets tumbling)
to the flicker of a flame
burnt the mantle black --
shadows melted
(moments) long ago
(but not so) far...

finished
before the start became
an end was writ...
I never understood...
in the quiet still
before I find you (first)
I breathe,
The world
that I remember...
is again...
a feather swept
(across) my soul;
words uttered to silence;

this -
memory of yet to be
and the smell
of burning pine...

bittersweet

I am memory
bittersweet my salvation
nothing matters more

you will choose for me
a moment of wondrous
o'er a lifetime less

silken dew on green
petals opened and waiting
the essence of life

pitch black the midnight
stars fade in comparison
uncertain return

the dying despair
curse my fragile existence
regret for my touch

were reason to be
to return without knowing
where I shall linger

what seasons to pass
but a glimmer of flame burned
for love remembered

immortality
I am the taste of summer
drying on parched lips

(one) Kentucky

I've seen my share
(was home to) bluer pastures...
seen fences (rusted wire),
barns that rose from ashes
to the stars...
I've lost it all
beneath the blue
Kentucky (fell one summer...)
but still I see the stains
upon my fingers...
(the smell of winter hay)
will always be,
without the need for getting
over --
Was not a hurt (was waiting)
to be healed...
a moment to be filled
with something more...
There's no need
to carve another over this -
tis only one
Kentucky...only one
as this within my heart,
the weathered barn....
(filled with warm tonight)...

Wasn't love the same
yet I'm amazed
at those (who raise the match)...
would seal the scars
with tar and bind their eyes
from looking back...
Would deem all memories
(the same)...
and deep within
an emptiness (holds the only proof)

100

here love was kept...
a house no longer furnished
(piano no one plays)...

Names are never uttered
lest the pain become renewed...
tis a ritual
of painting (over everything)...
til truth is nothing more
and nothing (just the same)...

Only love remains -
one Kentucky (just as blue)
moments kept apart -
restored to pasture...
(September sun)...
Stars were never less
for their shining...
never dimmed (into the black)
on which they burn.....

The bluest grass
still grows beyond the
meadows (I can see)...
and love
will never be a place
to get beyond...
Forever (both)
become much dearer
(initials carved in wood)...
poems penned to leaves
(the scent of maple)...
a key returned
the tender world (of me)....

mingled with rust

I been thinking
that maybe what's left (is
what matters)
how hated these
blossoms
that smelled of citrine...
when I walk down the
path
past the fencepost (you
whittled)...
I wonder did you pass
while I slept...
(warm still the stones
where you lingered)...

wrapped in the colors of
Jupiter
where I couldn't
see...(you were gone)
did you take the seeds
I had saved for this
season
scattered them far
(without a thought)
for my grief...

did you write of the
berries
(you won't remember)...
did you breathe of the
silence
we shared (disbelief)...

some moments so fragile
I touch them so seldom...
might crush them

with sentiment (a life in-
between)...
still it's hard
when I know they're
(wrapped in white
linen)...
each day a bit further
from truth I have seen...

baby, this night is busy
with feeling...
I drift through the
shadows, and
it's this I recall...
me, sitting somewhere
awaiting
(your presence)...
your breath on my
shoulder...
your back (to the wall)...

when the years have
been spent,
that's what I'll remember,
the cutting of flowers...
the falling of leaves...
a rosary worn by the
pillow (I dreamed),
and a vase that fell from
my window
(today)....

pieces the color of
whiskey...
mingled with rust
(from my hands)...

before we're done

a purple dawn;
a bit of lace.........
a redbird bathes beside
my steps
lines of chatter strung
across the road;
tangled up....cords of
shining soldiers
storm beneath the
boxwood
a secret yet untold...

ribbon tied beyond my
reach
the cedar's furthest
tender...
snowflakes to the hottest
breath - July
and from the porch
swing,
I can hear forever turn...
can touch the ladle
(scooping up the stars)
where meaning glows
(flush against the sky)...

a startled hawk
awakened by the smell
of ancient winds
a rabbit chased across
an autumn sun...
I listen (quiet)
the story isn't over yet
another moon shall pass
before we're done...

wheat fields dry where
locust
play (love songs)
to the night...
whispers grow
within the briar (a life of
circumstance)
the porch swing sways
Venus turns (silent to the
black)
her waltz unknown -
the long night begs her
(dance)

moksha

so fine the pattern
painted by the universe...
(what I know) is often tempered
by what I've chosen
(there to see...)
denying every proof
(was proof required...)
echoes might have been
the mountain falling
(though even now, I swear...
I hear a robin sing)...

what mantra I remember
was it just a name (I'd spoke before)
or only in the place
(my mind perceives)...
when held your hands...
and took your breath (as mine)...
was providence succumb
to nothing more than moments (passed)
forever gone
(before forever knew)...

I've said before
love is what we choose
(to keep...)
would I choose to be a dreamer...
seeing poppies
bloom from stones
(or symphonies of light
within your smile)....
I've wondered (as I do)...
and wandered (more because)
between reality and somewhere
(else) created...

I used to know
the sound that maples made
(before the turning red...
before a branch was broke...
the forest burns)...
I used to know
every secret of the sycamore
(cicadas stormed across
a golden sky)...
of every sign
(lightning bugs have gone for good)...
how much the weight (a whisper)
for a sigh.......

I knew the reasons then...
(and still I love)

I knew the warmth
of autumn (in December)...
what silence said
no words could guarantee...

I knew the way to you...
(and I was me)...

divinity...
a moment (manifesting)...
tears of joy mistaken
(could have been the rain)...

am I a fool for this
(I choose for nothing more)...
holding on (becoming still)...
what of love
will choose to be (again)

beneath the water's glass

we were younger
than the cypress
that lined the shadowed banks...

would swing above
ourselves before we dropped
into the cool...
feeling every wonder
with sweet exhilaration
taking every breath
as were our last....

I don't know
what (it was that) made us stop...
might have been the rope
was broken or it became too cold
for treasure...
might have been the land
was bought (and sold again)...
fences needing mended...
could the creek (beyond the meadow)
have run dry...

how it is...(and how it seems)
these so many years (removed)
were they lost
before that summer came...(and went)
floating like the petals
of dogwood on the rapids...
before the winds could carry
us away...

we were holding hands
just below the water's
glass..
clutching fast to that
which mattered most...
cooling arms and legs
wrapped
about in evermore...
I remember still the taste
of blue (your lips....)
the blush of innocence
forever in your eyes...

how many days were
passed
drying on a bed (of
moss....)
sharing all that was
(what still might be)
days turned into nights...
clouds rolled into
dreams (could not
compare)
constellations.......you
knew them all
(forgave me everything)...

the sweetest sound...
flat rocks on the water
echoing our voices
(joined as one...)

was ne'er a time we
thought
our time together
something (more than)
special
ripples spread
(was just) as it was
meant....

was later on
discovering
how much was there (to
miss)
would be the only reason
I'd return...

a quiet place
the universe decided
(fate)
the world (was big
enough)
(for only this) I needed...

love became
the memory of coming
home
will hold me
when years have
passed...

two hands
beneath the water's glass

river of stones

the light
a fading glimmer
moments nearly gone...

coal oil streaks the lanterns
wick burns into flame...
we huddle in the hallway
wrapped in quilts
that aren't quite done
we'd torn them from the frames...
(no thought for keeping)
destiny (unfair)
when lonely comes...

forgotten now
the reasons
for each tiny (careful) stitch...
my fingers worn with blisters...
pieces cut
the shape of life...
the chosen knew...
a dying man just down the road
a baby planned for spring
whispered hope for seasons
you are mine
(and I your wife)...

quieted by the gloom
of war approaching...
every desperate word
(even death) has purpose when...
might tomorrow
come (much sooner)
and we (both) be lost
before the night's desire...(spent)
I promise my allegiance

(come again)

there's a silence
when pain cannot be measured
in goodbyes...
to make it past this day
(one more touch before you go)
would be enough --
to see again the iris
(by the barn...)
to hold a newborn calf
black as blue (against the snow)

we'll wonder
for time we have been wasting
would trade (ten thousand nights)
for moments here (before)
your fingers brush my face
with the powder blue
(of truth)...
your skin glows
ghostly white
(as seashells on the shore)...

clinging to every word
your eyes are speaking soft...
I shall hold you (here)
as long as you will stay...

I know the worst is waiting
just beyond the fence...
with each startled cry....your eyes
fill up with tears...

with every breath,
they carry you away...

with me.........

gonna change the world
by being...
one moment at a time
gonna pack my bags
(and hit the road)....
that highway sure does wind....
gonna make my way
beneath a ribbon
(fathers know my name)
gonna spend the night
(shall plant my feet) in places
I became...

wanna change the world
by being...
who I am is something more
and nothing less (in getting there)
(or someone else before)...
there is no right (how dare I think)
just the place I am today
shall always be...(but then)
tomorrow - another place I'll stay
I'll swim in waves
I mastered...some other sea
(I knew)...
will fold the sails (were left of me)...
unchartered lands (of youth)...

will sing (forgotten every note)
til words are claimed
by truth...
will drink of them (remember living tasted)
what 'is' (now) the only proof...
I'll walk the sands...

where once I died...(fell ill beneath the sun)
shall lift my broken body...
with this spirit
(I am one)...

shall watch above
my sleeping form...
stretched long a distant trail...
to be the watcher (and the stars...)
love where love prevails...
I'll find my way
back across eternity (it seems)...
will wait my sure arrival
tho mountains rise between...

will be the sun...
to bake the road...
and burn to sweat the breath I chose..
til I become the rain...(again)
summer blooms
beneath the snow......

til winter's come

it won't be long
til winter's come
the nights are getting longer now
I'm thinking
of the canning that must be done
will see me through
beyond December's (frozen) lace...

I wonder do I have
the wood to last
til springtime...might I be forced
to buy from the farmer
(down the way)...

I watch the sky...
(reading) the season coming
will be bitter...
might lose a tree or two
before the tulips bloom...

It's quiet
(the sound of April melting)...
there are those I know
won't see another year...
Loves I've held
may never know how much they meant
(bittersweet) dearer they've become
(and welcomed here...)

I think I'll make a day
of doing nothing much...
might walk along that ancient
path to pray...
(will take it slow)
remembering with all I am...

(was love)
the day you came...
the night you went away...

just as then (the moments since)
and moments in between...
even knowing you'd be gone,
(before I knew)
I find a tender joy
in recollection...
another day, (forever)
spent (with you)...

it's the time of year (forgiveness)...
grapes are straining
on the vine...
leaves have started turning...
soon will fall...
Crisp beneath my boots...
red and autumn (painted path)...
branches broken
souvenirs (wherever)
grace allows...

It won't be long
til winter's come...
the nights are getting longer
now...

sometimes (like this)

sometimes (I wish)
I could cradle the anguish
I held (for a moment)
but now seems (a waste...)
of logical choice
and loving reaction
(a storm cloud retreating)
a promise replaced...

I remember how cool
(cold) can't remember
you were when was something
you wanted (from me...)
would talk all night long
til you were done asking...
then turn from the
questions that kept
me from sleep...

I try (to remember)...
each harsh indecision...
what talk of forever
was leaving (instead)
I try (so hard)
to remember each splinter --
each critical mark on the page
(circled red)...
could I speak from my
soul (without being rejected)...
did I mean to use caps
instead of lines (writ to blue...)
did I mean to say love
when my heart was just breaking...

reminded of who I was first
(before you)

did I mean what I said...
(I know you'll remember),
was given when love
was fated to start...
I'll remember the waffles,
a walk along granite...
doors bent for numbers
(just moments apart...)

I wish I knew how...
to take hold (of nothing...)
to let go of always...
thought turned into verse
I wish I knew how...
to return every heartache;
would stay up all night
(my longing to curse...)

but I can't...(and I won't....)
it's not me (I'm wanting)...
forgetting myself...
to give you the blame...
love never meant us to barter...
for sorrows...

the hand (softly holding)
the reasons we came

who I am (still)
isn't wanting for more
than who I will be
(with memories of you)
love doesn't need
(another deserving)...

I'd love you again
as then (I still do)...

touching

how far
before we stop
and turn around
(gazed at something -- broken --
passed along before)
lost upon this road
(one way street)...
and nowhere to stop
can only see
how quickly the road is nearing
to an end...

for all we might have had
(no more the wish it might)...
til we've replaced
the dream...with acceptance
desire with plans
(will come again)...
started from the beginning
a road with miles (before)
and just beginning...

places (still) to turnaround...
stops along the beach
(we might have touched and didn't know)...
I'm sure I passed you walking
(you didn't see)...
how could you know....would we have known
was just one road
and it would blister our feet...
curve into ten thousand vast horizons...
stop (and start again)

burned black the blacktop
that melts into the midnight...
an all-night diner

lovers bruised in sleeping
there along the shoulder...without a map
(just the stars)...
and some forgotten idea
of how it ought to be...
where the road would lead
with lots of time
(to wander)....

the road remembers
the way we came before
though the signs have faded (now)...
and the beach (retreated)
from the shore...

the road we took
has forgotten the way
(turning 'round)...
headlights split the summer sky...
ants move in one direction...

would longing change (the view,)
with no place to stop
(and sit)...

come along now...
the road is fading...
into the light
of passersby...
(a place we loved)
before

sandstone

Tuesday
seems I can't remember
yesterday (wasn't much
to hold on to)...
I thought you knew
could have sworn I told
you
(when you let me go)...
was just a breath
a moment
passing through
(on our ways)...

the music played
stuck in repetition
(and we sang
along)...crying
until we knew
every word (some we
couldn't say)
notes would bring a tear
(even now she breaks my
heart)...

not so much
has happened...
(and yet it does)
between the turning of
the leaves,
petals opened
as love returns to seed...
I scan the woods
for strangers (eyes
remember),

some days are gone
and others take forever
(with them)...

the calendar
is moved (another page
torn away)...
numbers becoming
numbers
(something I should
remember)...
for only mine...

the hands
move much slower...
when I hold them (just as
then)...

seasons live
within the canyon (that is
I)...
time paints her colors
sandstone red...
memory sharpens
(recalled where the river
flowed)...

was yesterday...
(but how can I be sure)

Tuesday
(seems I can't....)

118

already

already
I miss your face...
that twinkle I knew
(you had me then)...
when reached with your tiny fist
and pulled my heart
into your own...
(I knew)
this day would come
before I was (ever) ready
(but you've been waiting)
and those wings
I helped to polish (helped to weave)
they will help you soar
to places far beyond
those I (might have) dreamed for you...
but always
when others see that twinkle...
they'll see a part of me...
that laughs (when you laugh)
that sighs (when you sigh....)

and in your life...(through your life)
what is best of me...
will find a place to be
(a place with you)...
the best of you....

I love you.......

past the time

I've kept the best
(forgiven) times
I should have known...
walked beyond
the places roads were
meant to be
(for time alone) I cannot
know
what faith will bring...
what bridge I might still
walk across...
I kept the map created...
(roads grown over)
was not for me to choose
(love) our only loss...

I've kept the key,
although the house
(no longer stands as
proof)...
was hope that kept
the pantry full (that
patched a falling roof)...
I kept the lace was spun
for me
and weaved of threads
(so rare) (so fine)...
I kept the land
the same (was kept of
me)........
the taste of summer
whiskey
early vine...

I kept the light

was burned (for you)
before the wires strung...
before the fireflies left
and progress came...
kept the vigil past the
time
(when wax was melted
somewhere else)...

a wind was heard...
(returned for me -
the whisper of your
name)

I've kept the moments
past the time
(I should have let them
go)...
still revel in the chill
of waters rushed up from
the well...

of secrets shared...
(only you could know...)

I've kept the letters (every
one)...
read until the creases
tore...
fingers smudged with ink
poems meant for me
a lifetime passed...(to
please)
(a moment more)...

beneath the bed...
a box is lined with
blue the shade of winter
tears....
a ribbon someone
made (from memory)...

it hurts me now...
(my only sin)
were souvenirs I
wasted...
longing fills the places
(once so dear)

I kept them all...
pieces smelled of cedar,
where black and white
was deeper than
promises we made
a path along a river
doesn't run here
(anymore)...
a canopy of
dogwood......branches
blessed
(our only) shade...

what I kept
is laden (breathed)
with sweet perfume...
a beveled glass
(treasure from a box of
soap)...
a hand the same (fit me)
lines from right to left...

a key that works
(when no one knows)...
a light remains (still
burning)
in these - immortal
places
(I have kept)

silent songbirds

once I dreamed
and you weren't there...
tempting me
(familiar shadows...)
I couldn't understand
even when I spoke your
name
you turned away
and all I knew was gone

the day drew on
and nighttime came...
no sooner than the morn
was come...
I struggled then to stay
awake
a moment more
before my fate to see...

I should have known
it should have been the
way
I'd seen...

how could I sleep
and keep my solace
safe...
I've grown so used
to waking...
with my tears (a pillow
stained)

every night
the best to find...
I reach across the bed

I dreamed
was in a place...
alone with the just the
melody
of days (to be)...
silent songbirds
circled sweet...
blush their cheeks
were pressed against my
night...

shadows shift...
midnight's (willing) hands
part the world
(a curtain veils...)
into this one,
the other spills...
and I am left to neither

words escape
echoing soft against
the fading light...
where in another place
the sun is rising...

and I am there...
(again)

unread pages

another time learned
a page unbent
as another turns
a few sweet words
and a memory makes
underlined with pencil
what might have been
(had I thought that way)
had I read ahead
would I have seen myself
lost in the writer's work
my fate revealed
in lonely plots unfolding
decision to wake (or dream)
already made
committed to chapter
as yet unread

a ghost in my house
death before dying
choice never was the reason
(for choice)
lazy mornings, light turned yellow
except for windows
beyond tries to break
buried in linen
flipping through passage
a journey (to journey's end)
where truth is so easy (to know)
what is wrong
but refusal to see (never was)

the story remembers
how it was to be me
what might have been (me)
had I known how that feels

Toronto

from your couch
facing north (Toronto)...
you write of beaches
someone else (their toes were burnt)...
you speak of blue umbrellas
broken shells within the surf...
a breath of salt
and ancient seas
(blown through your hair)...
a promise...

you talk about the rise
and fall...the way the shore
forgets the light
that reached across
a raging storm...

recalling how the gulls
would dance...sailing flags
(upon a breeze....)

it's not the same...
stories someone told
can't take the place
of twilight burning
through (a patch of sky...)
red could never say enough
to tell of all she knows...
the warmest rose;
a valentine...
blood the scent of bittersweet...
(dry the drink) was darkest
just before an eastern storm...

it's not the same
to speak of
love...unknowing
of its wonder....
to speak of how love feels
(it doesn't feel at all).....

could words describe
the world that only lovers
see
how close
might be to fairytales...
a hand can never hold...

what kiss could swear...
when silence sings so
easily
red could never
take the place of
beauty...(unaware)
an hourglass
could ne'er perceive of
time
along the shore...the
rush of sands
poured between our
fingers...
the taste of salt
(forevermore)
melted to mortal skin....

love needs only know
there is no other....
(quite the same)
no red as true...no
ancient
sea would share
the treasure of our
name...

tis not the years
remembers where we
walked
or why we came...
footprints washed
away....(still)
no less endearing (to the
shore....)

no less the red...
than once was love,
bloomed within the
darkness...
could not be writ....
from promise
facing north...

words (are only words)
could never tell

paper cuts

they say
nothing lasts forever
(that's so easy)
take a chance
before you know (your life is changed)
love is living where you've
found it (that's okay)
it's not so much the taking
it's the truth
you take away

you can leave
(you won't be lonely)
you can run
(the world won't know)
you can swear to the darkness
what might be
it won't be long before
again your leaving hurts
(as leaving will)
because you can't run away
from your soul

long nights
and I've come to witness
(how I burn)
when danced (lapis wings)
into the flame
I practice every loop
(silhouette of shadows waning)
black against the smoke
a dreamer's game
leaving this behind
won't change the taking

126

what will I believe
who am I

(believing just the same)
you can leave
(you won't be lonely)
you can run
(the world won't know)
you can swear to the darkness
what might be
it won't be long before
again your leaving hurts
(as leaving will)
because you can't run away
from your soul

paper cuts
reminders that I held too tight
moments crushed
within my grasp (holding on)
remember when
you said you loved me
how was I to know
love is love without the need
for promise
it doesn't need a place
(to make it so)

you can leave
(you won't be lonely)
you can run
(the world won't know)
you can swear to the darkness
what might be

never burned

rugs almost bare
splintered planks
tug at broken threads
initials pressed into
tender walls
nearly faded
recollection
(only those who know
would know)

windows filled
with web and wings
curs-ed expectations
(but the light shows
through)
exposing a leather chair
a maple rocker
blankets and quilts
housed photographs
empty no longer obvious
(covered with yesterday's
skin)

candles awaiting the leap
never burned
(never knew)
hands atop the mantle
remembered why
(decided)
silent marching
desperately sure
tomorrow will be more
(we'll remember)

all that is here
(negated abundance)
egyptian sheets
(scarlet sheer)
stillness treasured
for all that was (enough)
eyes closed
and there (the colors)

ten thousand
brilliant shades
(in the dark only grey)

laughter seeps through
yellowed walls
and I am (only) alone
to remember
(what is missing)

flow on

was once a cry
no more than a whisper
(to the breeze)
a fragile light
surrendered
(folded soft around the
trees)
was once a bloom
(tho) my essence
wasn't there
petals without memory
truth denied the will (to
care)

was once a feather
(broken) by the rage
I'd come to tame
battered by the branches
were once my home
(yet loved the same)
was once a touch so rare
(patterned by an angel
wing)
brief as silence
graced the dawn
(was for love)
our everything

was once a highway
carved into
the mountain's pass
red with clay
streaked by tears
(were not too proud to
last)
a rock became a pillow
I was there
(I watched you sleep)
was not much different
than I am today
witness (to) this truth
I seek

was once a lock of hair
weaved beneath a silver
cord
was once a verse
I couldn't place
(divine) each sacred
word)
was once a choice
to be (I chose)
and came (as love) again

was once a voice
I longed to hear
whispered to the wind

before the seed

amber stirs
in wheat and honey
fields we separated
from the wood
feathers red
were scarlet rippled
beat the branches
in search of love's
remains
forever (good)
you've been gone
since cotton grew
now there's only seed
forgotten how it felt
to understand
(forgotten how to live)

was love our only need
take my hand
remember how it felt
to hold
how it felt to know
everything was true
(enough)
where the road might
lead us
would we find our way
(again)
how it felt to look
into the eyes of evermore
where we were
still we are (the same)

neath a noon day
scorched
barely touching (words)
fireflies imagined
where you gazed into
the sun
flirting (without reason)
but to know
(we'd found the way)

was there we hid the
truth
love was free
but forgot to say
(would we have listened)
now we're here
in places we will (will to)
stay

but in that other place
beyond the amber wheat
the cotton sweats
and moths recall
the sounds of longing
(easy)

a bulb swings bare
in the barn
the smell of summer hay
words were never
meant to be (enough)
a touch was all
(it was)

but it took our breath
(took the hurt away)

holding somewhere (found)
beneath a silver band
where stars were mingled
between these locks
of silk (and dreams)
walnut roasted
warmed by the chance
(we'd have it all)
never thought
to turn away
never thought to be
(another place so true)

just enough
to keep another season
another time when cotton
won't seed the fields
(we'll come alone)
led by ancient memory
(of where we were)
and when the dark
is at its best
a lonely sound shall piece
the night (together)
and I'll recall
the winter promised
(by your eyes)
before the seed
was bloomed

had I known

had I known
the leaves would fall
I might have loved them
(less)
might have held them
close
beneath an autumn sky
(my gratefulness)
had I known eternity
wouldn't be that long (to
live)
might I have loved
without the want
for something more
(than mine to give)
would I have kissed the
tears
and dried them each
(within my grace)
held apart their tragedies
a far (and dreamless)
place

had I known the sun
would sink
before my time was
through
that the veil (I had
resisted)
would block the path (to
you)
might I have held you
(longer)

more than lifetimes
(come and gone)
would I have traded
my salvation - another
day (and nights to come)

had I known (how sweet)
the holding
might be the last (of
love's refrain)
would I have held (as if)
there was no forevermore
(parting) with nothing
more to gain
would the loss have been
negated
by a fleeting kiss -
the dawn (awakened
somewhere else)
a reminder (of our bliss)

had the time (was
passed) between
been shorter to define
what paths I might have
wandered
through a world
(divine)
might I have loved
as I had never loved
before
for all that love was
(promised me)
I'd stay a moment more

132

sightless

had I forgotten
(my soul recalls)
another time
was here before
we walked along this
same
dark cliff
headed for the same
sweet shore

had I forgotten
of my will
might rise (as then)
to choose my way
what shadows shall
remember me
when here again
(the path is laid)

what hand
will find me
(holding on)
shall guide me down
this rocky face
will catch me
when my sight has failed
would come as light
into this place

what story
will be ended (soon)
another (season) waits to
start

what truth was mine
(and left to be)
what heart (shall pulse)
within my heart

had I forgotten
words (revealed)
were left behind
to claim my pen
what name I knew
the same as mine
will be forgot
(when come again)

had I forgotten
moments (dear)
the way I warm
(against your voice)
will time return
itself to this
a path (designed)
forgotten choice

let arrows fly
directionless
and known
by only love (to will)
had I forgotten
when you came
how long I waited
(standing still)

133

weight of red

it won't be long
the trees
(already bending)
there's promise to the
wind
I never heard before
it tells me wait
begs me hold
a season (longer)
but I see the leaves
such lovely shades (of
red)
cracked beneath my feet
(bare and brown)

the sun is lower now
than yesterday
I can't see beyond
what plans were made
(and left) for us (undone)
threads have turned
to silver (from chestnut
weaved)
cotton worn so thin
I see right thru

familiar path
now broken by
roots (rushed) to ground
were searching for a
place
they knew back then

I see the way
they strain
(above the worried dirt)
I envy how they love
never holding back

was here when leaves
were green
and blossoms filled the
sky
essence fell
(swirling blades)
rain upon the day
poems were brand new
(and eager to be read)
I never thought
the blooms would
fade to fall (so quickly)

the stillness breaks
bothered by the dream
(we never slept)
petals rise
(dancing melodies)
swirled along the roots
(strained to remember
this)
another day
the leaves were young
(and feet were bare
and brown)

same sweet world

between the times
(I remember clear)
there are times
(places still)
I go
(would linger for a little
while)
returned with faith
(all I can hold)
I lie awake
on cotton sheets
journeyed far
to a world (unknown)
I might have been
and there, am still
content with this
(to dream alone)

unnoticed
by the anxious clock
whose silent hands
around me move
moments counted
(rare and sweet)
have not a debt (with me)
to prove

just the same
(no less for touch)
would tender need
a place to fall
I'll wait
til silence speaks again
I'll watch the night
(move) down the hall

in times between
and days recalled
seasons pass
and nothing's changed
for here (is there)
and there (I am)
no less for longing
rearranged

was not for lack of will
(I pray)
was love made more
by time (asleep)
the place I go
not far from here
the same sweet world
(a place I keep)

half full

I've forgotten
what I dreamed of
was but a girl (one day)
with want for more than
fairytales and knights
(of polished steel...)

for this
the picket fence
and rooms where silence
(wonders)
would trade (it all)
for touch
that I'd remember
long past the time
my skin was cooled
the sky no longer
blue

one kiss
by which the rest
might (never) understand
would hold
(the girl I was)
til a woman came

what point now
in broken lines of living
for what (tomorrow)
has not sense (to worry)
was only good enough

when the best
I've known
will hold me (still)
when nothing else
(remembers)
one time
one dream
another lifetime waiting
destiny and canyons
dwelled between

for still a girl (was I)
returning for the one
was meant to find
and I a memory speaking
(remember)

truth (out loud)

the darkness folds
brittle arms
surround me here
(I kneel)
to ask for this
(no more)
but that I will endure
for no one else
(but you)

only you
can know (of me)
(here) in this place
where just your light
pervades my soul
not so much
you'd never know
how much (how little)
I (might) take
and make it more

held to me
a simple spark
webs of silver flame
and fire spreads
til in my (little) voice
I speak
what I (alone) can hear

trembled lips
denied a (louder) voice
surrender this
who would know
what name
I give (to love)

what silence (will) I know
without words to say

for only this
(said aloud) immortality

with your name
upon my breath
truth is spilled (to light)

upon the water

waiting
for prophecy spoke before
was not our time
(to understand)
words placed in bottles
and cast upon the waters

returning now
echoes
as was (and still)
(at last) I can tell
what before I could not
say (never understood)
how truth
was in the seeking
weakness (becomes)
our strength
where once I had not voice
a whisper (cries)
beyond the noise

forgotten (was) the day
we turned
(unknowing)
and cast our words
upon the sea

mothballs

til this day
I had forgotten
moments stored away
to sacred shadows
I come alone
longing fingers trace
along scarlet threads
pieces bound
together (love) only here
would I have
kept them (mine)

hand-written notes
maps and magazines
half empty bottles of
bourbon
starched a blue shirt
(buttons strained for
touch)
words recalled to rhyme
sang again (the proof)
we were
but for a place
forever wanted
another sun
(hope)
for what we had sworn

hushed low beneath a fall
(of winter ash)
water washed away
tears I might have seen
(believed for me)
fairytales are told again
(graced with wonder)
of why we came
for only this (and
moments more
the way) uncertain

questions asked
and answered (in the
asking)
secrets stitched
(unknowing)
into pieces
(we were then)
meaning
yet unweaved
(and stored in cedar
crypts)

hissing

beyond the rain
who will know (of this)

a morning came
before the red could rise
while others slept
I planted (sorrows) beyond the gate
and watched them bloom
purple and frail
bent (just so) to steal
the falling dew

all was quiet
save for one
who spied from trees
beyond the well
(curs'ed I would turn)
my name so low it fell
hissing

many times
(swallows circling)
and nothing there
just the moon's
reflecting (moments)
across a puddled path
where I saw the face of love
(ten thousand times)
smiled before the sun
awoke

hours will pass
and no one will know
(it rained)

fated winds

were this the way
(forever) spent
and others passed
for us (before)
I'd wonder if our love
was true
(or only meant
for something more)
moments waited us to
find
the meaning (why) was
left undone
a star embraced the
rising sun
was promise clear
(another night to come)

how far away (from here)
I've been
through the darkness
(turned to day)
traveled lonely roads
alone
seeking signs
along the way
I've wandered back
this way (as then)
stood and watched
(you wait for me)
understood the way
(I should)
closed my eyes
afraid to see

days passed by
(before I slept)
moments melted into
years
words forgotten
(but by love)
joy remains despite the
tears
praise I give
for I am blessed
bliss was mine (shall I
atone)....

and make a lifetime
out of this
the choice to come
(to this - my home)

another dawn
(decides the truth)
where every past
has been erased
but for this touch
(I'd come anew)
fated winds my soul to
grace
a name so sweet (I hear it
now)
just the same (I love it so)
memories
awaiting (still)
e'er we return
this love (to know)

closer to the stars

you stayed away
much longer than you meant
but I was waiting
near the window
(you could see me from the road)
and everything was still
the same
though years have bent
us both
but something there
is just as it had been (before)
and moments keep no pictures
of the past

I'd thought a time or two
of where you might have gone
did you make it to that diner
stayed up all night long
(to dance)
what engine held you closer
than I ever could
did you long for me
(forgiveness)
beneath a desert moon

I remember hearing
somewhere
you had lost your faith
and for nights
I prayed and worried of the road before
when ere a storm would come
I'd speak your name (aloud)
and stare out at the darkness
everywhere (and wondering)

it's been a while
the place don't look the same
(as then)
the orchard fell a year or so ago
the old porch swing
still sways
(beneath the weight of memory)
there's some things I don't say
(I wish I could)

come inside
I've got some coffee brewing
what pride I may have had
was lost in yesterday
there are latches need replacing
and fields now gone (to seed)

I moved the bed
much closer to the window
I can lie awake
and count the stars
(you gave to me)

nothing's changed
tho time has passed
(winters without asking)
no need to say
I've never locked the door
some might call me crazy
but most are gone from here

most all my life
I've waited for this day
you stayed away
much longer than you meant

turned crimson

twilight burned
against a sky turned crimson
laced with ash

I stood beneath the snow
eyes closed
against the heat
and thought of all was lost
(but here they were)
mingled with november
and fell to pieces

paneling
ruined by crayon
green and brown plaid
hand-me-down drapes

carpet worn thin
by tiny brown feet
windows the color of nothing
clear to the touch
cold to the world (looking in)
looking out
clothes on the line
the yard had grown smaller
a miniature likeness
of a place I had loved
the knob fit the same
in my hand

would now be gone
and I not the only one (missing)
destinies cheated
of these

stories told
by flashlight
tents from dining tables
whispering laughter
eyes expectant with questions
held these
the hands of no longer
covered with black

evermore moans
as flame finds the roof
windows shattered
by rain
(not enough)
to forgive what the wind
has decided

pages from my
yesterdays
my heart can't help
but wonder
how long til I forget

leaves curl
with liquid blue smoke
dancing
through the night
wings softer than needed
to carry my past
away

and I will go

morning
and the earth is new
come with me
beyond the stillness
the old path worn down
two apart
and side by side
lined with cedars
and swells of autumn lust
the glistening lake
take me there
fill me with sunshine
laugh and I'll remember
this (and nothing less)
our words will fade
into the trees
kiss every tower
with brittle pines and
budding cones
skim the paddles
row by row
ripples wash
across scales of silver
to your waiting smile

mine is the memory
when you turn
an open hand,
to let me hold it,
and the silence knows
I will

pages (bare)

why should i care
what words were mine
and what were come
for others (meant)
what slant of ink
or curve of loop
would choose for me
a verse unspent
what darling dropped
below the line
or verse returned
(a place to be)
was found a place
with thought to give
was rhyme unmatched
when left with me

why should i care
what would i know
(how dare i think)
this purpose mine
would choose for letters
long since lost
and given use
before my time
why should i cling
to page and pen
with grief for words
now stole away
remembered how it felt
(to write)
would prose defend
or love betray

why should i care
when i am gone
would silence share
these thoughts i keep
forgotten how
this treasure came
(as prayers to night
or dreams to sleep)
why should i care
but still i do
for words unwritten
my truth shall tell
when i am left
to pages (bare)
what stranger then
shall know me well

lullaby

there was a time
I wondered
at the silence (I could
hear)
even when the night
was all around
it would speak to me
so clear
I wondered how
and wondered why
it was my fate
to hear you then
with words I could not
understand
you'd breathe my name
(again)

was played
with every cricket's tune
every brush of luna wing
each falling star
a vow would make
another night to bring
I'd hear you
in the morning blades
softest sigh
before the dew
lullaby of longing
sweetest song (I ever
knew)

in stillness (I remember)
there's promise on the
breeze
in petals (still unfolding)
in the crunch of autumn
leaves
in the whitest snow
where shadows glisten
(every flake to shine)

I hear your words (come
with me)
every memory (every
time)

some nights
I roll the windows down
and listen for your voice
miles from roads we
traveled on
forgiven every choice
and always (there)
I find you
calling softly (just the
same)
above the sound of
living

I hear (the music
of) my name

another just the same

tis mystery to others
guess they wonder
where I'm going
my bags are packed
with things I used to
wear
I'm eating less
and dreaming more
(as longing seeks a place
to be)
some nights I walk
for distances
I never knew I could
so rarely I recall
the choice between

I knew the storm
was coming before
the thunder did
could see tomorrow
blazing in your eyes
I couldn't look
(preferred the future
take me by surprise)
I waded barefoot
through the creek
that ran beside a stand of
oak
traced bleeding hands
across the proof of us

I'm living still
in places unrequited
still wear the same
old dress (a shade of
aubergine)

tendrils come unfastened
silver earrings
brush my skin
I'm everywhere
and nowhere (long
enough
to stay)

the blueberries
are bluer than they were
before
and not far from the path
mourning doves have
built a home
he watches from the
tallest branch
and whispers of forever
each time I turn
I hear his loving song

for every moment
different
there's another
just the same
and love would not be
love
if it were something less
where melodies
were written
from memory (much
sweeter)

evermore is closer
than the night

149

rounding the bend

comes the turning
cycles (jaded)
by the summer sun
days burdened with regret
retreating shadows
when stars were wished upon
did they imagine this
(I'm sure they know)
it won't be long til white is white
and angels will be lost
within the snow
soon will be the glistening
of the moon against their masks
their truth (held captive)
beneath the cold

the hours into dark
stole away her longing sighs bathed in sweat
tomorrow shall remember
and grieve (again) for days
of twisted knots
on golden skin
promise of another
moment filled with longing
(calls from distant shores)
and a prayer
for cooler nights

my horoscope
decided by an empty page
lines for me to fill
before these autumn leaves
I hold you in my arms
tho already late (the cooling kiss)
I close my eyes

and hear
the church bells ring
beyond the blue
of stillness
another spring
shall think of us
alone for just one winter
and nothing more to do
even silence knew
(to let us be)

I hold my breath
imagining another time
where once a candle
burned
a junebug in July
the jar is almost empty
where the light was held
and the song
that filled the sky
is floated (far) away

one yellow flicker
lingers where the others
flew - a halo left
the only sign
they loved

past forgiving

the fields
were past forgiving
forgotten how it felt to drink
would that they grow
in shade along
the (southern) fence
was not for me to say
not for me to choose
(I would)
who should come inside
reprieve for sorrows
suffering
(but for a little while)

there were no words
for thirst
much more than love
we couldn't ask
I held your head
against my breaking heart
and cooled your ragged lips
with tears

(too old for crying)

but for a moment
there was no other place
a world that moved between
the time we shared
(we'll share again)
(will I remember this)

lord please help me (understand)
there's more than us
more than crops

would save us from
the losses (ours to keep)
and others
we have known

I wonder
can you see me
do you smell the dogwood blooms
(of summertime)
what comfort these my hands
will make for you
(do you know)
your shirt is torn
but still the blue
becomes your eyes
and all I see
are skies beyond the cotton
(we should have flown)

listen now
(I won't say much
of anything)
we're expecting storms
tonight
I'll hold you near (til then)
will rock you as the
thunder booms
everything
will be alright

just close your eyes
and dream
(of rushing rivers)
I'll wake you
when the tin roof
starts to cry

re-written

here is a song
I never could sing
was riddled with words
I can't say
was penned to my hand
(one night in the dark)
its meaning unknown
til this day

this is a dream
I can't understand
of a house somewhere
I never lived
black and white
souvenirs
hand-me-down pieces
each leaving (one more)
to forgive

there is a path
that winds through the
wood - down past the
barn to the glen
littered with buttercups
ivy and root
she knows every
(sweet) might have been

where is the moon
a season passed by
through lifetimes and joy
burned (the same)
ripples of circumstance
tides rise (from falling)
as the universe loves
without shame

deep in my soul
eternity hides
the key to places I love
blossoms once bursting
returning (in time) to be
the garden
(I never knew of)

this is the tree
I climbed as a child
still remembers the
warmth
of my hand
gave me a canopy
of ruby and green
shared every future
I planned

here is a page
could never know all
thought without courage
to write
lines could not witness
what the soul cannot say
dreams held apart
from the light

this is a promise
I've been waiting to keep
was writ to these hands
(long ago)
held between leaves
a red and green canopy
and words to a song
I don't know

yellow daisies

i broke your plate
beneath the dirty water
was a moment
that i held onto
wanting everything
to wait (awhile) for me
when couldn't be
(so much has changed)
how much of me
already gone

it's not the same
(as then)
some nights i eat alone
with just the missing
and the sounds
that keep the night
beyond
this old screen door
forever watches from the
trees
he stole my favorite
sheets
(the yellow daisies)

i found him dreaming
there beneath the stars
were meant for us
i begged him go
my sorrow (not for
anyone)
he swore he would
but i know he's sleeping
(somewhere)
i raise my head
as a tender flame is
caught
the water running (red)
i see him there
wrapped in summertime
and crying now
for me

the moon in the pond

i dreamed
and somewhere
it was snowing
the air was so crisp
you could see thoughts
(become)
but poppies were burst
through cracks in the ice
and clover was
buried in evergreen
branches (sparkling
ornaments rang through
the night)

my shoes were too tight
lights were reflected
with the moon in the
pond
stars knew (where to fall)
silence grieved
the loss of the crickets
(so) heavy the wanting
of winter

i picked at the poppies
a handful of verses
kept warm by my breath
and pressed to my heart
i walked past the days
of melting and sorrow
love was i taking
somewhere
far away

fields were just turned
the earth's rich perfume
filled every hope
with reason to keep
the poppies had wilted
but red was their reason
what fool would believe
what remained
of the seed

the sun found me
dreaming
(a dream of a dreamer)
barefooted daughter
this keeper of truths
the clothing of winter
piled high in the shadows
lying in splendor
of rapture's red blossom
tears of remember
reflected to blue

eternity started

what more
could you tell me
of all that I know
would move me to wonder
wherein I was lost
what web I survived to weave
to this place
tis nothing the heart could
remember

of all I have known
I'd learn it anew
blind to the storm
restored by the rain
held in the arms (eternity started)
would learn to breathe
all over

what faults made you real
more than dreams to a poet
holding on (still)
to that which I know to be more
(than verses, and rhyme,
seasons and stories)
remorse has no claim
on redemption
silence no proof of a lie

if e'er I could choose
given now (as I do)
to breathe (just as easy as then)
I am held by a truth
tis greater than I

every moment
I love you (again)

autumn breeze

when I am left
as ashes cast
unto an autumn breeze
will in your heart
a music play
each tender note of me
will every word
be written
to the part of you (was
mine)
would grief erase the
memory
of all these tender times

when silver vines
have taken o'er
the garden's gentle lace
and dark the breath
of winter
has cooled our last
embrace
e'er weeping
be the only proof of love
I knew
give to every branch
the gifts (of love)
I gave to you

when I have left
and pages (lonely)
seek one more refrain
lines were barely written
will be remembered
not again
will then I fall
some mystery
that no one cared to tell
where ash has blown
and words are all that's
left
of me - then shall
you speak of love
that loved you well

parchment grey

parchment grey
with silver lines
to keep your words
(from straying)
letters always
found their way
beyond the captive page
into my soul

faceless color stained my
hands
my skin a stranger
until then
another marker made
a scar the shade of
raven's silk
(black, your favorite
drink)
escaped from thought
(the strongest bars
became)
parchment could not sell
(what he couldn't say)
the message fell
where understanding
(knew)

another choice
(remember)
would not believe
at all

folded thrice
the same (but now the
creases worn)
til words that held so
tight
have come apart
pieces of the scribe
given thought (and loving
hand)
served their master well
but now lie lonely
for words that didn't
come
black that stains
a lover's place
lines between (apart)

confessions need
no place to fall
no lines to lean upon
without the words
(returned)
I still would know
for in the places tender
(ink could never find a
way)
a language there is
understood
(forever written)
needs not
the parchment page
or lines another drew

(they couldn't hear)

was yesterday
and I mourned the loss
the dreamers
had stopped dreaming
what lives were trapped
beyond the night
were screaming for release

(they couldn't hear)
they slept through to morn
and wondered where the hours went
(so rested from their beds)
not a sigh was left
no feathers on the pillows
wet footprints on the floor
the night before
and nothing changed at all

there was no aching
to know what might have been
(or what already is
and I can't hold it)
there were no midnight calls to someone else
(please tell me you're okay)
no begging one more chance - one more time
(one more day)

the pages became emptier
for there was nothing
left to write
all was it was meant to be
just this and nothing more
yesterday no more
than chapters given to the flame
the past not even passed
(no more to hold onto)

the night (sospiro)
no more the promise
of stars, no more than light
the place between
where lovers sometimes meet
was just a fairytale
and all the destinies
that weren't written
were lost
(and no one even knew
their name)

was yesterday
and I mourned the loss

the dreamers
had stopped dreaming

I never knew

forever came and went
yet somewhere in the
mirror
I see its shimmer
(just the same)
a reflection of "I know"
(I never did)

with my palm
against the sheen
stretched to meet my
own
another world beyond
(beside)
the one I hold
so different
just the same (warmer)

a world familiar
what is this place
we hold onto
just a portion
of eternity (we choose to
go)
into another us
much nearer to the truth
than we could say
we keep

(silent remembering)

then just when I believe
I've started over
I pass along
a stretch of glass
a curve of polished
chrome
(and there she is)
the woman
I am too
belonging to the places
where she lives
(where she loves)

(where she loves)

odd familiarity
I gaze into the knowing
longing seeks
to understand
the me I never knew

enchufla

born without the eyes
I need to see
beyond the choice for
love
purpose and promises
left to be (was I)
to choose
(was love returned for
less)
when tiny hands
are raised
fists came back with air
(blue against the
clutching)
til someone came for me
armed against the
demons
(I had) summoned here

I understand
though how long un-
remembering
how long before to find
photographs painted
(hid)
beneath these dark
eyelids
to feel my way
naked to the dark
compelled
I dance

surrounded by the arms
(I know but where)
just as real
as I allow them be
mystery becomes
a favored waltz
(warm breath
against my cheek)

moments
float and sway
ignorance (no more than
I)
a momentary
(madness)
essence (the ghost of
destiny)
lingered from my long-
ago
reminders (here is more
than here)
I have no time to keep
only to seek
was known before we
were
partial to the reasons
I chose this place (to be)

was not for truth alone
I came (to dance)

raining (scarlet)

have you forgotten
everything you knew (before)
of scarlet leaves
pirouetted blaze into the sky
swirling dancers
majestic in their graceful fall
the chill that grows to
warn the heart of winter's edge
forgotten how the night
(so long)
was sweeter to recall

have you forgotten
how the music swelled
when there was nothing there
no melody to hear
no songs of you and me
notes replayed (from life's desire)
no hymn that some might sing
when we have gone (away)
the beat of someone else's drum
the flame another fire

have you forgotten
how each word would thrill
and in the silence
(all your longing freed)
your mind could touch
each line of hope
(even now you swear it's true)
was torture each awaiting
just to hear them breathe

if wonder
you've forgotten
then there's nothing left

to fear
the leaves
will never float that way again
and what of flame
will only burn til lost
the need for air
moments such as these
though near (immortal)
may never be again
(and yet) somewhere

I close my eyes
and leaves are raining (scarlet)
a chorus none can hear
I hear them yet
wherever solitude becomes
another drum is beating
embers glow
til all I see (is what I know)

the universe remembers
(how could I forget)

a moment's stain

last night I walked
though I can't recall
how far from here
the hours passed
(was years but just a
minute)
beyond the rise
a valley spread
(turning gold the death
of summer)

more than once
a barn was lit and there
was rest - before to go
I don't know where
somebody's child
was called a name
I didn't know
(for a moment almost
waking)

the north had moved
from where I knew
planets shifted within my
sleep (so close I raised
my hand
and burned my fingers)

everything I heard
at once
though none but I was
keeping there
the splash of green
against my skin
a flower cried
(as I held her close)

we mourned the season's
turning into places far
away (I still remember)

the way
the laughter echoed
off the mirrored lake
smiles (the shade
of grape snow cones)
quilts were spread
beneath
the budding trees
locust strummed
in melody
secrets
we would strain to hear
and not so far away
the waters rippled
(as yesterday
looked back at me)

it's just the same
I saw it all last night
tho places
seemed much smaller
than the wonder (I recall)
how dark
each moment's stain
(will we uncover)
much deeper than the
blood
(was never gone)
and not so far a walk
beyond the season's
passed
somebody's child
was called a name
I didn't know

166

reaches for the red

wake me up before
the blooms have burst
against
the dawn
before the final star
has fallen softly with the
dew
til every wish is gone
and light becomes the
place
that was the moon
I was there
(eternity)
with dreams already
started

wake me up before
tequila reaches for the
red
before regret is come
(courting yesterday)
before the only thing
that's left
is memory of the longing
wake me up so I may sit
with each goodbye
broken shells (kisses on
the shore)
before the tides are
turned
into tomorrow

wake me up
while destiny is sleeping
before my fate decided
by the hours in between
let me warm myself
against
the want for evermore
held within his brief
embrace
midnight blankets
wrapped around

wake me up before
the sun has slipped
(between the
covers)
stealing every memory
(of how we loved)
before the petals open
sleepy heads unto the
day
before I turn to
find him (nearly gone)

wake me up

167

along the way

was left from here
so very far (the ways I've come)
from the yesterday
(I muddled through)
tomorrow plans I never should
have made
from the windows blur
every truth I've told
every place I've loved
is passed along the way

empty pockets
and moments to remember
I never wanted
numbered pages
filled with souvenirs and ink
(their meaning come undone)
trust that told of nothing
but goodbye

it's a long way back
I'm almost sure we'd never go
if the bus would turn around
what would we do
we'll cry for us
for the innocence (we thought)
was part of living
now we see was just
a part of love (we never knew)

I've slept most all the night
tho silence sometimes woke me
from the towns worn in between
another life
(gone by)

I searched the night for you
a place you might be waiting
for a ride

this road
(runs on and on)
been winding
most my days and half my nights
through broken towns
and neon slats
a canyon through the years
(whistling) as rubber left the black
lighting up a world
beyond the glass

a murmured sigh
longing whispered (from a dream)
is nothing but the music
of the way
(a road somewhere)
I'm traveling alone
forgotten (now)
the reasons why I came
but up ahead
the morning must have come
to cheat the night
of places (still to go)

# of flying

comfort settles
along the edge of the
floor
just below the joint
where the wall would
meet
it's enough to drive you
crazy
suffocation (I've heard it
called)
a fog spreading (honey)
to every splintered board
every missing nail
touching, loving,
warming intoxication

sweeter brandy
could not be than this
erasing every past
every worried heart
every far away
you dreamed of
trading places with
worlds
you might have died for
(once)

til all you know
(is this)
nothing more could you
recall

not even the moment
it happened
(there a mist across the
boards)
ready to run
you turned and took a
seat
as easy then
(o it isn't any more)
now you sit
unable to move beyond
webs you gave into
(inviting)
fog still burns you
breathing
ache that knows your
name

clings to every piece
of you remembered

curves along your spine
holding (as a lover would)
tracing warmth
amid the scars
you can't recall (their
coming)
some far away you traded
before this was
a memory (of flying)

no one goes

all day I sleep
in rooms
where no one goes
tucked away the grown
up clothes
(I should have worn)
tis all a waste
for nakedness is my
resolve
shall crush the pillow to
these
mortal blossoms
cushions weighted
holy remnants (of sin)

at night, I
wander......white and
pale
beneath the daunting
sliver of half awake
eyelids drawn (shutters
on the world)
there's no one here to
watch
no one will ever know I
left the room
would never shake
the sinner's sheets
(to find me gone)

chocolates and day old
sweets
news someone thought
we ought to know

but now the print is
faded
(rained just yesterday)
I'd forgotten they
delivered
(wonder who has all the
rest)

in solitude, I search for
papers
'lest love be lost
were not for me (the story
known)
cups cracked with
broken pencils
ink puddled in disgrace
(festering) reminders
of truth I should have
written
nights before

all day I sleep
in rose papered rooms
remembered
unremembering
a vision caught between
the lace
and glass
is hardly known
but for me still lingers
(where no one sees)
watching for the faintest
hint
I know of my nakedness

fell as feathers

feathers floated
end to end
raven black to winter white
tumbled on a breeze
her continents displaced
by words a lover swore
(far away seems nothing
more than reasons)
change is coming
ice already melting
from their caps
too soon the slightest distance
will be forgotten

will poinsettias bloom
before easter comes
shall I hold these truths
were left for me
somewhere (I should have been)
were growing in my garden
while I was watching
skies above
seeds were sown
(I never saw them watered)
when petals fell
were feathers I had known

ring of seaglass

I wonder what love
will remember of me
worn flannel gowns
long nights on the porch
stars (merged with pieces
of wing)
stirred with lemon
a ring of sea glass
echoes and mist
wrapped through the
trees
light flickered there past
the night

mandolin strings
were aching to sing
(a warm bowl of soup
I never could eat)
my eyes fixed on
something
retreating
lanterns strung from
evergreen boughs
silver becoming
in puzzles of blue

I wonder what love
will remember of me
was there in the shadows
the shades of forever
love was forgiven
of all that would come

taken communion
(manna so sweet)
to seek understanding
the ways we had come
and go back to living
(tho never the same)

where witnessed the
moon
who envied for touch
but swore to keep secret
the truth

bare feet crossing
warm weathered boards
drank from the same
piece of glass
spoke with eyes
(with much more to say)
but couldn't remember
the promises
(meant to be) made

I wonder what love
will remember of me
when rolled to my back
and sailed out to sea
when wisdom is shot
through the night (on a
stem)
would flame as prism
extinguished by dreams

reminders to believe

what fate for me
decided
this life to resurrect
what eager page
could never still my pen
what kindness
was much softer
than I remembered (now)
somewhere before
(for this) was left
to verse

I've charted
constellations
across an early sky
much greater their reflection
was the memory
of your eyes
what smile the taste
of winter snow
was meant to make me weep
paths no longer open
to my shoes

sooner then
the coming back
(no less) for twilights spent
waiting for a star to fall again
held aloft by (stronger) arms
could never understand
my need to be (alone)
but not so far apart
from then

the time between
was agony
(but nothing else made sense)
was all I knew of love
more than death
these hands could keep
was for a moment (more)
I traded this
the way unknown
where waiting
I shall find the wonder
just as I did then
when nights are lost
and lonely sits upon my bed
will lilies turn
remembering my smile

where shadows
dust the ceiling
yesterday is shaded black
while pieces of my memory
crowd around the candle's flame
I lie here in the darkness
begging destiny to come
this place to love
this night (another dawn to fill)

buckets carried from the well
burdened by my prayer
will love remember
something more of me
than yesterdays now gone
a wind without a home
keeps the words I left for me
reminders to believe
more than love (was love)
I came back for

life song

T'was years before
I wanted
another truth
(another)
but for this;
through days and lifetimes
wandered past the places
life left lonely
from taking back
(and wanting more)
than wrong made right.

I walked in darkness
(though it was day)
lost and looking
for a light,
a truth,
a hand to hold.

Was faded (fated too ...)
I'd find a way
and wake one day
in-different eyes,
hearing words and one else
would hear
each sunrise.
Held my breath
(understanding)
what worlds were
there without.
I cursed
(so long the days)
standing still
and filled
with doubt.

Light within
a thousand suns
still couldn't see
the veil of tears
beyond,
where other paths
we might be called,
and speak aloud
in sacred voice
a solemn vow
(who didn't know my
name)
whose path was sure
and for a time
the journey proved the
same.

Springtime seasons
bloomed
a rare and radiant seed
beyond this life,
another dream
as loving hearts decreed.
When asked redemption
given us
and something less,
a hand to hold,
a fire to tend,
a secret unconfessed.
Was never lost
forgotten when
to keep
what dreams then knew
before;
we ever felt the need
to end desire,
to sleep.

Then was I lost
(but for a while)
a flame burned unaware,
reflected me within your
eyes
might find my purpose
there?
Or woven in the quoted
verse
and scripture
I looked for signs
in what was left
yet never looked
within ourselves
for heaven here
on Earth.

'round me fell

was just passing through
without a plan to be
never meant to find
another piece
of me
was only looking back
where I had passed
before
one last look around
might show me
what I came here for

was just walking through
back across the day
when I heard a song
another time I'd played
it was the same sweet
sound
echoes around me fell
memories I'd left to die
I never told them all
there was that time
I cried
there was the time
I lived
was the night I knew
you'd come
no matter where
I went

it all seems foolish now
what did I think I'd do

would find the way was
here
when only passing
through
would find the meaning
(new)
somehow
to understand
every word made clear
longing whispered
to the wind

was just passing through
your hand was waving
high
in places
still I keep
the sun has gone;
the stars are bright
it's not the way it was
was wandered here
before
touched by
familiar light
I still remember you

I was just passing
through
when the music played
before the night sailed on

the moon against
the waves

washed away my name

here you are
the same
tho something more
(than then)
grown restless
where the truth was (hid)
some green
was growing purple when
the road was new
a ribbon
wound into the black

we dreamed in shifts
all we had
rolled upon our back
we'd find the rest
planned to
change the world
(someday)
would give them more
than they imagined
(more than we
could say)

we traced the webs
between the stars
counted stones and steps
fourteen hundred thirty
two
before the sun was dry
most nights
was not another there
silent but for tears
(the crickets cried)
for days we walked
forgotten

by the need to speak
language came undone
in circles
(never missed)

your boots were old
before we ever started
(did we choose)
but fit you like the grey
beneath your brow

a crooked smile
broke my compass
(every time)
would take your hand
and wade into
unknowing
rivers cold as blue
washed my name away

time was nothing (more)
than one direction
how far to the nearest
feather bed - a postcard
held the world in little
pieces
the rest could see
(not enough to
understand)
more we wouldn't give

the universe
was painted ours
and sworn to never tell
lies beneath a postmark
four days old

I dreamed

I dreamed
and the meadow was empty
(no one buried in
ashes below)
the girls were dressed in yellow
I sewed them
and buttons smiles had become
dolls and soldiers
marched in a line
beneath holly boughs
and evergreen branch
(sashes)
the colors of freedom
flying
stars fell on pages
of blue
all and still
(as it had been)
restored the start
on forever
there you were
walking
with snow on your shoulders
flowers bloomed
from your hand (daffodils)

painted blue

I can't explain
the way the world
was given me
kaleidoscope
of reds and green
(painted blue)
the sunrise shades
my favored ink
while twilight keeps
a count of words
(that rhyme)

the night bird sings
all day long
sits outside my window
sill
(forgotten where he was
and what he meant
to do)
he waits for me
as I awaited him
(come to me)
a promise to fulfill

the silence cloaks
familiar sound
my own soft
murmuring
of songs (I wish I knew)
melodies I love
are played as sweet
would others hear
(come to me)
and long
to know the truth

the wind
he carries me
to places far away
no need for dreams
(the morning comes too
soon)
etched upon my soul
every word I never heard
a poem given me
tomorrow's moon

I breathe
and for a moment
I've returned again
(come to me)
and let the judgment wait
for colors
I'm becoming
orchid, lapis blue and red

red as poppies
growing by the gate
blue the shade
of night before the
morning stirs
green
the moon's reflection
to the sun

I wait in colors
yet to be discovered
I close my eyes
and hear the night bird
sing

rusted clean

my father's father
made the bed
we married on
was pieced together
feather stuck between
the sheets
a slanted bit of paint
and the date was kept
nothing much
(but getting by)
never thought we slept
lonely nights gone by
a whisper outside the door
let me go when I
couldn't stay
begged me stay when
I should have run
beyond the fence
beyond the pasture's graze
where destiny
had come
taking the best along
summer filled with blue
smoke so thick
I (cried)
couldn't see you there
wouldn't have been (for me)
the last
the best forgave (again)
loneliness came for me
when every night
was long
when the creek was dry
the ladle rusted clean
I slept out on the porch
rather than watch you leave

over Jordan

a savior came
to slay my sorrow
(secrets of my
emptiness)
a lover came
to share my longing
saved a many night
from rest

past the time
of resurrection
forever smells
of kerosene
lacey aprons
weaved with worry
lamps alight
with flame (unseen)

colors tell
the time for reaping
but what of me (I have no say)
would speak
to change the sun's
direction
what need could write
the storms away

raise the river
over Jordan
death can never claim
my pen
when shadows come
to steal my presence
words will speak
to silence then

183

somewhere (the same)

I took a walk
the night was cool
somewhere else
a gentle snow
was melted by my memory
where was I going (I don't know)
seasons come
(forgotten read)
life resumes (leaves still fall)
the past can never
be (let go)
the past is never
passed at all

forgotten reason
stranger things
harsher truths
(than this) we told
once I wrote
words I can't recall
pieced together
(held soft) against my soul

I took a walk
beyond the reach of night
even angels
had come to see
snow drifting
lace into light
burning (somewhere)
might have been
I pass between
the stars
(one with love)
light burns beneath
my skin

go again

was past the need
for choosing
when I chose again
(take me back)
no memory
remained of
what you said
(what I heard)
was only that (desire)
a need to search
of wonder why
and when
to understand
reasons I would
choose (to choose) again

roads before
and trials between
paths took me near
(and o so far)
rural roads
and tin roofs
boxes nailed upon a
tree
a river flowed too fast
(had I forgotten
how blue your kiss)
I waded in
teased by leaves
were spinning by
pieces left (I couldn't
place)

held me there
sad as sails
(the color of jasper)
pulled beneath

somewhere the waters
ripple
a lonely vow
(I can't recall)
stretching clear and deep
polished proof
of time (the river)
not as young
as it was then
leaves fell from branches
of the tree where
first we loved

lost from where they
came
they go (again)

lonely they give to me

the morning sun
she blinds
bounces off
passing cars
life goes while I
stand still
wonders if I ever will
falls once on open eyes
before they look away
it's the only same
every time I wait
wish I didn't need
lonely
others give to me
emptiness I know
has nowhere else to go
falls once on open eyes
before they look away

won't be long
before the chill
puts up another fence
frosted
on my side
safe every truth I hide
pain I couldn't share
goes with me
everywhere
falls once on open eyes
before they look away
too much of me

is gone
nights barely holding on
was yesterday
I place I even knew
wouldn't know
falls once on open eyes
before they look away

a crumpled dollar sails
before the light
turns green
eyes search but
never see
the world forgotten then
no time to comprehend
falls once on open eyes
before they look away
I wasn't always here
a prisoner
to my fears
once I had my dreams
faded now the days
between
sometimes remembered
when
I was just like them
falls once on open eyes
before they look away

the morning sun
she burns

stones

I thought of you
but not for long
what beauty you have
come to prize
what majesty was
painted purple
far from me
another lies

of changes
surely this will be
and you will choose
the same again
shall turn your cheek
before I see you crying
tears were not for words
you held within

of sentinels
we courted
echoed steps on sheets
of grey
fixed as schools of ravens
wings upturned
and forced to pray

for solitude
and secrets hid
where no one would
believe
shared and never
thought to hold
gave and never thought
to grieve

I thought of you
as I have thought
of others gone before
chasing down some
dream
might never be
ages into ages
I was never meant to stay
forever holds the door
ajar for me

longing speaks
like whispers on a grave
at night
no one hears but those
who have no say
purpose left to prophets
moss to claim a lover's
kiss
death without a reason
to delay

I thought of you
as on the wall the lonely
raven
spoke of loss
stones were facing east
another blazing sun
warmed the bed
where lovers slept
with dreams of evermore
stilled their misery
eternity begun

better still

better that the dream
be gone
than held for me
one moment more
that breath should heave
one final sigh
(a whisper of surrender)
so I would know
its sweetness
as every wind
that blows

better that the seeds
be tossed
to highways (not yet
walked along)
wed in painted canyons
pressed to meadows
bloomed with frost
upon the forest floor
where rain was fallen
(softly)
yesterday

better that my soul
remember
what of beauty came
and where each wonder
lingered
(did I know)
with every kindness
(not forgotten)
every smile
a kiss forgave

better that I wait
for day to come
without a light I meant
to keep
(windows glowing bright)
across the sands,
the night
where is my love

better I believe
in everafter
(surely come)
eternity I would wish
and wait another lifetime
(remember me)
where meadows bloom
from seeds
today I grieved

188

who's to say

You gave of touch
and promised moments,
(more than time)
as grace allowed.
I gave a kiss
and of the words I hadn't
learned
I'd find them all
(somehow).
You gave me silence
held in treasure;
the stillness of a sigh.
I gave you breath
was once so easy;
lifetimes passed
(yet here am I).

You gave me pause,
pushed my mind
to question without end;
to find the worth
in wonder - the light
where light began.
I gave you faith
o'er every mountain
standing in your way;
saw you stronger
than you might have
been
(but who's to say).

You gave me blue
to sail the night,
steel to skate a frozen
pond.
I gave you red,
poppies (slept) beneath
a noonday sun.
For every star you traced
(in locks)
beneath a stand of pines,
you gave me paths
of mystery,
were truths (already
mine).

You gave me love
would reach beyond
what promise we might
hold
(til then).
I gave you love
was never yours to
choose
(it has no end).
You gave me more
than I could tell;
much more than words
(as these) can show -

 a will to write,
a place to fall,
a calm to still
my soul.

somewhere else

from the porch
I hear the leaves
are drying
somewhere else
the wind (forgets)
wrestles with the past
yellow falls the first
and waits for red
to match the way
he circles to the ground

pieces caught up
in the rush to end
autumn comes
with ruby moon
silver rakes
through naked limbs
where yesterday
was summer
everybody said
another wind would blow

pieces left
from that first
night of spring
petals pushed
beneath the snow
came too early
to remember us
(the way the sunlight
glistened in your hair)
soft the touch
of make believe
a walk along the path
before the porch
was here

I remember
just how good it was
to dream (we dreamed)
beneath these same sweet stars
before the spring
had come
blossoms
to block the view

wrapped in pieces
pieces ripped
from blue and grey
flannel tied with red
cords of maple
wool and satin
everything made sense
(fitting near)
without the words
to make it so
held our wishes
still within (silent)
as they fell (for us)
tossing silver into red

intimacies of autumn
wrapped in pieces
left of spring
remembers still
the words (I love you)
never made a sound
now they do
leaves are falling

again
I see the stars

purple roads

you choose the road
I'm driving
sit there for a while
and close your eyes
o honey
wait until we get there
long before the sun comes up
still warm enough
through the night
I'll watch the headlights
casting lacey spells
upon your sleeping face
hid in shadows (I believe)
was wonder made

forget the map
it never made for sense
whenever choice was come
direction always seems to know
the universe deciding
(purple roads)
turn around or stop
to watch us spinning
long deserted strands
white lines fading
into no one knows
(which way to where we're going)
forever held within
as far as we can reach
before the dream
wakes up

it'll be your turn
to drive

death a fool

I've wondered how it was
you could speak
and know my name
whispered in unknowing
rang a chord
I heard the same
as once I did
another place
though muffled by the
veil
was spoke as tears
were falling
another telling
now to tell

I've wandered
waiting (torn apart)
for pieces to return
thought erased in
coming back
new reason to be learned
I've grown impatient
leaving
tis only love I understand
the part of us
familiar
as lines
across my hand

as longing
was a heartbeat
memories of letting go

no different now
than when we loved
did parting make it so
would make again
the choice
before the flesh could
ever cool
believing love immortal
would prove of death
a fool

I've wondered when
the time was right
have chose and chosen
well
breathed with breath
forgotten now
in darkness woke the
bell,
broke the seal of dreams
was given
and held to truth (so
dear)
beyond this veil of
wondering
(the voice the love)
I hear

memory of rain

the cycle returning
as red light to cinder
a place near enough
i learn to begin
and wanted for more
than moments could give
more than these colors
black and blue ribbons
shadows another
October
the color of clay
washed out by living
came as we dreamed
(far away floating)
swept us away

til nothing was left
but waves on the grass
rocks once we grew
oleander
fences now fallen
the boards could not
hold
one more nail
we would give it
and begging to stand
would hold all we had
gathered a lifetime
(together)

no longer the fields
burdened with cotton
we might stand at the
edge

filling bags
with our reasons
but we can't stop forever
from falling
we can't stall
the memory of rain

soaked to the skin
drunk with forgetfulness
for one yesterday
I'd give up the fight
to float as a tiny
white blossom to sail
(spinning)
past everything
(I remember)

to wake
without dreaming of land
a place somewhere
(far)
past returning
water unfaithful
as truth into seed

remember love

before these hands
are stilled
and the world is stopped
will you
know me (then)
when there's nothing
here to keep you
(dis-believing)

will you
speak my name
when there's no one
left to hear
(who will remember love)
when silence warms
blankets
that I used to keep
when the fire was gone
ashes held
a fragile truth
(the only proof)
we lived
where the wood
was piled
cedar between cedars
deeper than the roots
(were left beneath)
years stacked up
on years

paper mountains
woodsmoke drifted
on the winds
where used to blow
a momentary chill

skates on moonlight
(just long enough)
this keeping
past the time
I should have listened
when you warned
me go
(so much I didn't know)
I'll never know

embers flare
shadows race along the
wall
smoke to dry
these eyes
of long ago reflecting
redbird eyes
were the dreams
that slumber sold

before the cedars fell
before the valley
cried beneath the weight
of smoke
as mist poured green
upon the lake
summer loved

will they ever know
the truth
was smelled of cedar
when comes the time
at last
you speak my name

dimensions

the sky
was growing
dark
autumn shortened by the
cold
someone knew
the way
but couldn't make it
in the dark
I knew just where to turn
how many trees
how many bumps
of missing road
had me
turned around
stars we left unwished
(another night)
were glad
to shine the way
awaiting
when I found
the house
wrapped in vine
and washed with light
fanned as flame to wing
flickering visions
to glitter swam
a slope of black
against a darker night
fireflies (thousands)
how could I not have
seen
another presence here
I swear
the air is easier

and music (something)
no it's not imagination
though I know
it could be enough
might trick me into
dancing
tho I don't know the song
is one I've heard
one we used
to love
played over and over
a spinning dream
pressed
in plastic (starts again)
he couldn't play
but no one really cared
and now they've changed
the place
til no one knows (to
know)
he'd be humbled
by the way
they've made magic
of his sound
assuming
it's not me
(a melody trapped inside)
everyone is hushed
the music softer
they look at me
and again (I wonder)
was I ever here
are they only waiting
me to dance

for tomorrow's sun

were only there
one star left shining
one wish
and I the first to see
the last to know
would not for once
a wealth imagine
or more
than years already
passed
would not for fame
I trade misfortune
or take from thee
these fathers
still to shine

would ask no more
than that which
I can never know for sure
that you would know
before your
road was ended
the world revealed
in me
was first a flame
within your eyes
reflection of all I
could be (becoming)
I saw myself
as you could only see
(saw you
as only I)

I wish (and then)
would places be revealed
where I could hide
the truth
words could be
persuaded to be much
more
than words
would tell you
everything (you seek
to know)
resolved in beauty
(was fault her wonder)
the sorrow
of goodbye
the mystery
our hello

would not for me
a star be lost
nor faint for light
I never made
but for tomorrow's
sun
you might be waiting
(still)
I'd make a wish
and (gladly) take his
place

happenstance

what yesterday
decided
of tomorrows
we shall know
had the winter
ended sooner
would they have had a son
a moment later
years ahead
and every now is changed
nights when fate was meant to come
another knew instead
with eyes
though not the same
and for me waited
called to me another name
I never had
but for a star that made its way
past mercury and mars
was past the call to war
the angels came
speaking of a place
not yet imagined
a world was dreamed
and waiting us
as hands moved slowly
'cross the sands
given more to
happenstance
than we could ever know
to find in this
arriving
back to us
we wandered home

tears for no reason

women break easily
time after time
it's the one
that is leaving
we miss (by design)
a lifetime of struggle
which fight
do we choose

fighting to love
or fighting to lose

I've wondered
so long
why love feels this way
tears
for no reason
and nights melt away
where truth used to swim
sheets sweated
by word
couldn't be more
(we wanted much more)

than silence (the
answers)
we heard

what evermore waited
now settles for this
a moment forgotten
the taste of a kiss

I do what I do
and he does
what he will
the same was good
sometimes
(a memory still)
we fell into something
no longer the same
yesterday
fated to shadows

(and no one to blame)

what we couldn't know
we've learned to ignore
what's the point
when we don't touch
the same as before
forever is left
being broken
(wondering where the
ending begins)
just the way
we remembered
the moon
as hands holding
soft (was that love)
breaking in

a smile unkept

when I was empty
you moved my aching
heart
to thunder
through the clouds
a face I knew
smiled and everything
was as was meant to be
a fool to doubt
a fool to wonder
when there was no need
o please
I never needed ask
you knew my words
before I willed
them speak
for years I hid
in places now forgotten
trading trust
for recompense
evermore no more than
this
a place to be
as I would need another
more than me
a sun beyond my own
was just a flame
reflection fading in your
eyes
where once I bathed
hours into night
where only you could see
beauty (owed to you)

was my belief
the water filled with
pearls
(ten thousand tears)
so grievous the notion
that a smile
unmeant for love
would tarry as the last
proof of passion shared
that my skin
ashamed in glowing
would forget the silken
touch of breath
before the storm
the warmth of water
rising (as canyons form)
pools of understanding
love needs only (truth)
to be love
as I would give
not waiting absolution
(for moments)
when the clouds
appeared
(as rainbow colors)
freedom really free
as I decide
was meant to be (was I)
before -
before was something
less
caused my heart to doubt
awaiting this permission
(to be love)

christopher

with yellow green
you created skies
where once before
kites rehearsed
tails of tattered ribbon
chose for us a better flight
swirls of red burst (proud)
against the blue
a dragon once
a sailor sworn allegiance
to his ship
would sail no less
amazed as these
(and christopher before)
open eyes
undaunted by the sun
watchers from worlds
below (and far)
where nimble fingers
pull and push
against the wind's resolve

silent wood

in shadows
were the drummers hid
silver arrows
pierced the green
stood watch above
the lovers
seldom heard
their music played
stood aside
as sighs were traded
words undone
by twilight's glow
prayed awhile for something more
(would never be)
to change the world
moved aside these stones
til there be nothing
left (to show the way)
a path became a fortress
brought and kept us (here)
lessons thought we learned
but had no memory
of hours spent
(waiting in the dark)
before the morning
gave for us
another drum
a heartbeat rose
against the archer's mark
no longer only watching
arrows rained
as silence listened
grateful
for the shadows

dimpled red

there's a scar
that has no memory
of what the hurt was
done
or pain that didn't bleed
before I knew of me
it paints a darker
blush across my skin
used to be my focus
every time
I lingered
was the proof
of (imperfection)
my mystery

never thought
of battles won (or lost)
without a sword to wield
only love was raised
no scars
were burned
to what could never be
(remembered)
this confession
hides a hurt
no one can see

from a loving hand
another cut
much deeper than
was love that held
(it open)

fingers trace
the dimpled red
sensitive to touch
(longing numb
as flame chased hot
across the snow)

was nothing
said of me
witness to the wound(ed
soul)
others might have seen
words that left their mark
before the rest
was known

the truth remains
(in places you can't see)
reminders need not
wear the scars
of love

dreams of this

were words
I'd spoke before
and so I spoke them
(new)
again
was no one
there to listen
'cept the raindrops
on the glass
the last of autumn
colors
melted somewhere to the
east
I could hear the first
flakes falling
as I drifted
off to sleep

wrapped in ashes
cedar smoke
feathers thick upon
my breast
song that cooled
when met with change
enough to keep me close
drifting elsewhere
beyond the frost
patterns to the panes
left my ribbons
to show the way
returning
how long til they'd
be covered
up in dreams

familiar warmth
of made believe
almost frozen
by the fall
the coming back
much harder than it
should have been
lips turned blue
as winters fell
forgotten
how to kiss
and wrapped in wool
(muted shades of red)
stitched while I was
sleeping
far away in dreams
of this

cherry blossom

when cherry blossoms
scraped against the grass
so heavy was the burden
that I stepped around
walking as I would
(without the benefit of rain)
and miles
from where the story started
something caught between
I stumped my toe
on circumstance
never saw it coming
til was gone
waiting (watching)
holding high the lantern
would spill as candle
to the flame
fill the dark
with light of somewhere else
(pull the curtain back)
let the blossoms scream
a garden
not for me the going went
or where was I before
(you never saw)
the path I took
and led you long
into the world was us
(I miss it so)
how to find my way
back there to this
crawled into the drink
was cherry blossoms
reaching for the light
that was my love

constellation

was chosen well
the time to come
and split the word
divine
the wherewithal
resentment
for the seekers
yet to find
and waiting idle
where the shades
of grey
were bled to black
that bid a season passed
we never knew
he'd take us back
or ever would (in turning)
see another
passed beyond
into the place
where dreams are kept
(I've wondered for so
long)
of choices left for making
(love forgotten by your
heart)
converged
into a distant star
and rolled against the
dark
tho others buried deep
in places (still)
would dare to speak
as came for us

ten thousand drums
to beat the plains
between
and never wept
for those whose song
is buried in her bosom
safe

tribes no longer
bound by blood together
without sound
without a name
and not a one
remembers them
(came to understand)
to meet as strangers
in the vale
birth to birth (and hand
to hand)
what little me
what more for I
would choose the road
they knew
and wander as the past
(into the light)
was light pursued
this only this
no more for me
or you (you can't decide)
I will not ask
(I could not ask)
why they would shine
tonight

echoes

stillness weights
in autumn air
the echoed ghosts
of honey bees
the moon's reflection
broken not by blossoms
nor by leaves
sits heavy on the fog
circled neath
a wingless form
might cold keep him
anchored by the memory
of the hive
empty now of cursing
without regard for prayers
(too late)
where she remaining
queen (is still)
as sworn to honor
watches o'er sleeping soldiers
wherein her lust
swarms silent

he said she said

he said
she said
but no one thought
to listen

couldn't hear the raging river
torrents of the heart
and no one knew
what he was saying
sometimes words
cannot be uttered
couldn't bear to know the worst

was the hurt
of letting go
when he wanted
(to hold on)
but hers the fault
he had to manage
couldn't tell the truth
was taking
from the soul she earned
the one she held

as close
the shade of blue
that hides Kentucky
and shines a frozen pond
from eyes
that never stopped
to look away
never had the strength
was a world
so close

just there as they were dancing
he closed them then
as she did too

but for a moment
opened wide
to somewhere (far away)

living
they might never know
(couldn't speak)
but knew it all
no way to change it back
to unsee what was seen
what was given
dared the truth to disbelieve
he couldn't do
she'd never need to ask

was only love (no more)
would make up rules to mask
the way it was
would listen as
each bell (in silence ringing)
moments slipped away
into stories
they would tell
(someday forgotten)
was the way they fit together
hand to hand
and mouth to mouth
a kiss to seal each word
they'd never speak

he said
she said
but no one thought
to listen

echoes

stillness weights
in autumn air
the echoed ghosts
of honey bees
the moon's reflection
broken not by blossoms
nor by leaves
sits heavy on the fog
circled neath
a wingless form
might cold keep him
anchored by the memory
of the hive
empty now of cursing
without regard for prayers
(too late)
where she remaining
queen (is still)
as sworn to honor
watches o'er sleeping soldiers
wherein her lust
swarms silent

quarry

forever was so very far
and not for me
to know
sequestered by the want
that rules my soul
and waiting for a knock
that might have come
I can't be sure
was meant for me to
answer
meant for me to hear
the quiet conversation
a lover's lament
the water drumming soft
against the roof
forgotten tears wash
aside
the flailing tin
as certain of another life
beyond the falling rain
I missed you

when the storm was
raging
thunder spoke your
name
never heard you knock
were not for petals
left behind
I'd wonder if you ever
passed at all
but the comfort feels
as if you were
could be I was dreaming
I'm not sure

did I put my arms
around you
did I beg you come to bed
did I hold you for a
moment
(maybe longer than
before)

pancakes and a spot of
tea
did I sing
(I sometimes do)
were the curtains pulled
around to block the
traitor sun
were the windows opened
wide to catch the rain

I wish I could remember
the quarry of your eyes
the berry of your lips
the way your hand
fit mine

with every storm
that comes
I stand outside the door
when thunder begs
redemption,
so do I
as lightening spills
her longing to the dark
I see you there
beyond the reach
of night

to be understood

Life In-Between

He said.

Let me ask you something,
If you don't mind.
Lay my head on your shoulder
Wrap myself in your storm,
Where it's safe
Where it's warm.
Let me tell you something.
I promise it's something real.
Let me tell you something,
Something about myself.
Something I've never told a soul
Not even myself
Out of fear
Out of the knowledge I wouldn't be understood,
Known
Confirming my solitude
Confirming I'm alone.

I'm a middle aged, middle child
Born to middle class means,
In the middle of a country
That values extremes.
I don't know what that means
If anything
In the greater scheme
If anything,
But I do know
I do believe
I'm happiest in my middle life,
That world I find between.
Between the absurdity of the waking world

And the lucid world of dreams
Where anything is possible
And nothing is what it seems.
There lies the creative world
Combining the two.
There I find that amazing world
That led me straight to you.

She said.

I'm from another place
just south
and to the east
most all my days
spent barefoot
'cept those
spent on my knees
'cept those I walked
within the darkness
searching for a light
would burn
with me
the brighter
of suns within the night
written word
and followed maps
we made of yesterday
across the plains
o'er other sands
would lead me back
this way
from middle
to the north
south of everything
your road
a gravel lane
you chiseled every rock
were steps (to where I'm going)

a path to bring me home

He said.

So here we are.
A fortuitous interlude
Where life fades away
Concerns and fear allay
Dreams and visions hold sway.
An oasis
In the midst of this convoluted jungle.
Temperate winds
Beneath a sky so blue.
But it's not like us to savor the moment
It's not like us to let time slip by
Unexamined, unquestioned.
So we search the drifting clouds
For purpose,
For meaning.
But it's up to us to provide that meaning,
Wouldn't you agree?
Meaning is the gift we give
Purpose the reason we survive, we live?

She said.

There's so much more
than this,
a life to spend
in search of bliss
as sighs held captive
to a kiss...
begin to give us answer.
There's wings
with light their only truth,
days behind we hid the proof,
gave the best to wasted youth,
knew we'd come to nothing.

Let's just pretend
for a moment now
we're in this place
as fate allowed,
will find our way to truth
(somehow),
much stronger for the journey.

She said, it's no more
than a day
just close your eyes
and know the way
is open where we left before
the same we came
to follow...

close your eyes
reach out your hand
there's much
that I don't understand
but I'll show you what I do
and then...
when we have passed
into the light
we'll remember this
(redeeming night)
when truth bespoke
of wisdom's plight
was here we lingered
out of sight
an oasis
for the moment

He said.

You make me laugh
At myself
At the simplicity of it all.
Why did I make it so
complicated?
When it was as plain and
true and beautiful
As you
And this moment.
This moment.

So long I've wandered
So long I've searched
Desperate to find reason
To conquer why
To slay doubt
And all the while
It was here
In your arms.

The only truth
The only meaning,
The only reason,
To love and be loved.
No matter how briefly.
How deeply.

How lovely.

She said.

was not for you decided
I never asked
(how could I ask)
when was always mine
to give (to hold)
however brief
(eternity shall pass
and start all over)
was not for you decided
I never asked
(why would I ask).

into the sun

hours passing
yellow beams on
hardwood floors
ghosts of something
(talked about)
finds a way to give us
more
finds reason
in the waiting
for passing winds
our truth to hear
what we love
of us becoming
came again
and folded near
shades are pulled
and music beckons
might we glide
to songs of old
clutching hands
against our bosom
distant voices
still our soul
might I have been
the gaze of fancy
far away and held you
tight
as we were spinning
beneath the lantern
where venus blazed
by candlelight

I loved you then
will love you ever
forgotten steps
but warmth the same
faint the breath
that tells of heaven
shall take this dance
and others claim

red becomes
the sailor's sunrise
black a sweeter shade
of blue
skies were clouded
(I never saw them)
was drifting neath
the world of you

miles and rivers
eternal nothing
would count in breaths
the days between
love need not
be lost at sunset
'tis more than this
a moment dreamed

early frost

darling
December is pressing
(I feel it)
no less than a chill
i can't see the sun
scratched was a heart
on the glass
by your name
time unremembered
words come
undone

i wrote you a letter
another one scattered
by winds of no longer
words we don't say
how can it be
love finds us always
last night
i dreamed
my way back to you

we were walking
somewhere
with no need for talking
so much to discover
nothing to know
a lifetime of drifting
hands told the story
warm in the telling
but harder to hold

truth is no less
for secrets unspoken
would love look away
or choose
to disguise
I wonder at silence
(the universe listens)
I hear with my soul
nothing left
of goodbye

this morning
a stag was waiting
my coming
i told him to go
(i don't know
what he heard)

more

there's more to me than this
you see
through eyes afraid of seeing more
more than tears
were fallen
I left somewhere behind
where you won't know
you can't imagine
tender there
between the thorns
hope within the stone
rivers deeper
than the flame
you think is gone
yet burns
where you can't see
orchids bloomed
with raven wings
and fireflies fill the night

more than might have been
I am

passed in the hall

was startled
by a dream
(pieces falling into place)
a promise
given clarity
as evermore to grace

from birth
a quest for wisdom
came questions still to ask
such pleasure
with the asking
each mystery surpassed

and tho the house
was empty
but for birds along the
wall
(they couldn't sing)
they wouldn't sing
were frightened by it all

so taken
by insanity
at last I knew the rest
what pages had been missing
scripture burned
of consequence
when someone chose
for others
what each should choose alone
would take you there
if mine to do
would gladly lead you home

I couldn't sleep
the hours passed
as shadows rearrange
what longing knew
his way around
was truth I wouldn't change
always here
I see that now
I'd looked for
someone else
was sleeping on my pillow
searching for myself

twas always here
(I wonder)
who was the woman
in the shawl
did I share this fate
with breakfast
a night bird strained
to call
who watched me
from a distance
storied arms
too weak to fight
taken down forsaken paths
in shadows of the night

approaching dawn
was Tennessee
far beyond my fears
wallpaper birds now gather
these sacred psalms
to share

leaning

when every vow
at last is kept
and broken just the same
when no one knows
the reasons past
we wait love's sweet refrain
in making up
and make believe
choosing sides
and placing blame
the last one picked
the first one gone
and no one
knew your name

if I had known
might I have been
much kinder to defend
would pull the broken
from the grave
and hold you high again
might I have given breath
another mother's son
might I have loved
and lost
the same as times
I lost and won

I've wandered roads
I might have missed
found love in souls divine
held a baby to my breast
another life - and time
were pieces held
in meadows dark

222

and canons loud and mean

holding life within my hands
as death flowed in between

wouldn't change a thing
wouldn't trade that day
for thousands more than ten
would dance while death
was playing
e'er the band strike up again
and call my name
from all the others
waiting for their place
would fall into the arms
I know
my first (my last)
embrace

black and white
now faded grey
and sworn to thankfulness
in memory of a walk beyond
was brought my path to bliss
when held apart
for moments
knew would never be the same
as there beneath
the redbuds bloom
when whispered soft your name

you promised me the dance
if I would promise you
the song
what vows still wait
becoming
forever takes so long
forever takes so long

edges

there were miles
before we knew
for more
than mountains
didn't know the world
beyond our porch
beyond our piece of land
those who loved
we loved them back
were wondered
when we couldn't
wander far

dreamed but
there were limits
to imagining
miles were covered
rivers ran but
who could know
of pools and falls
between
watched as spinning
petals disappeared

were some
we held for moments
then let them go
never saw them coming
home
or knew for what they
loved (wondering)
did they ever
think to turnaround
to speak our name aloud
was a mile too far
ten thousand more the
same
was too long
coming back
without the wisdom
of the roads

how many nights
with only stars to guide
how many miles
were not for us
to know

sweet familiar

I've grown accustomed
to the way
this house
moans beneath my feet
nights I come awake
to hear her weeping
she tends
her broken heart
away from windows
so sure within the night
not one can see

but for me
(and I know better)
I hear her suffered sighs
her curs-ed lot
when the day is barely
young
how many petals fade
beyond her (empty) porch
the roof no longer
witness to her crying
awaits the day
(tomorrow) brings her
down

sorrow watches from
the window
nearly every night
while
yesterday lies sleeping
in a bed beneath
the floor

between lace and light

without the world
to witness
caught between
the lace and light
lost to places
I had always known

a touch remembered
loving kindness
willed to warmth in
ancient pools
and more than that
a day or two of whiskers
a smile worn red by
questioning
imagined both
and blushed
(they burned)
my skin

to turn away
hiding all I knew
(and wanting to know
more)
avoiding now my rush
to explanations
why the leaves were not
yet
falling
the summer stayed so
long

songs erupted high
above the trees
males declaring season
hope for endless love
as ravens coupled
tumbled from
the highest perch
(forgotten for a moment
they could fly)

covered every path
might lead me home
but this I knew
enough to fill my longing
undiscovered
hidden pieces (buried) of
my past
a keeper now (I am)
of paradise

simplistic

would that I could tell
and make them listen
those who make from
worry
ammunition
war to trade
and no one understands
why the battle
rages on and on
but I do

it's not so hard
to comprehend
couldn't be an answer
easier to question
what bullet could
conceive
another bullet
from a prayer
what canon's roar
could drown the sound
of evergreens
what fire could rage
within the mind where
love was never kept
who would notice
when it burned
out of control
who would ever see
from ashes
where the story changed
when it might have been
and were we
meant to serve

mistaken gods

another game to play
too many aces
left to fall
never understood
the way to win
was just to walk away

how simple
I must seem
to those who make the
plans
who worry o'er designs
as to what the winner
wins
who gets the blame
who gets to claim the
victor for himself
when day is done
who gets to sleep
without the weight of
sorrow
he unleashed
without the weight
of sons forgotten
beneath the meadow
deep enough
to hold them all
their simple truth
forgotten

who of us shall cry
for them

wish again

break the ribbon
tied each thought
close your eyes
and count to ten
make your wishes
til now unspoken
close your eyes
(wish again)
for only years
no more these moments
kept the best
to trade for now
purple satin and red organza
linen folded 'round somehow
you wondered
almost waiting
wished for moments
taken back
to pass again
another name
of those your father
lacked
your mother lied
each time she swore
to fulfill your destiny
what was it that she said
but for you
she'd always be

still you knew
you chose her
so many others (given love)
chosen sweet
her summer dresses
spread with periwinkle buds

228

you chose but fought
this new becoming
as another waking promise
passed
from life to dust
decided by the universe
sworn before the first
to be the last
of candles flamed
your name repeated
softer
somewhere else (to light)
quiet reverie
two lovers contemplated
how the world could change
if only

if only they could
see through other eyes
was the first they knew
first truth
they recognized
a place beyond
the one they lived
hush repeated then
secrets turned to wing
as breath to skin
arms wrapped
each around
reflection of the one
together made
somewhere they wouldn't be
(but still)
they knew
ribbons
would be broken
wishes made

geese against the moon

the time is past
for waking in the twilight
for dreaming
without eyes to see the
way
for ages been
and I remembered them
all new
but it's not the same
(I'm not the same)
as you
(remember me)
maybe we were meant
and coming from
different paths
walking took us (always)
back to something (once
we had)
we let go
and now I wonder
was it magic (just that
day)
was it wonder
I carried with me
finally I could see
in your eyes
my own reflection pooled
on frozen ponds
(the geese were landing
there)
silhouettes painted to
silver moons

wings brushed into
quietness
not for me to spoil
whispers echoed in
between
in places (still)

I miss you
when the sky is chilled
and morning cools
to rain within my heart
just before the dawn
when silver
leaves have fallen
(I remember)

will you understand
what words
I'm still without
looking back
through places now I see
again
wondering if you loved
me
makes no difference
now (you love me)
this who I am
you might not recognize
but for this
love's reflection
(in my eyes)

no one knew to tell

not much time
has passed
though much
(forever) changed
about this place
remembered when
I painted these
cedar red
the yard a little bigger
and the house sat farther
back
was miles away
a little girl
(with knobby knees)
dropped below
the highest branch
squeals to
fill the space between
the back porch
and the barn

mystery
was more than us
the (wasted) world
beyond
no one knew to tell
had never been
(and come back better)
flowers of another kind
burst to flame
on southern wings
(names no longer spoken)
never known
not much to hold

even less to care
what suffering might wait
beyond the broken fence
left tracks
to be discovered
others taken by regret
couldn't see
what still was coming
wouldn't change
a thing

days were longer
years beyond the reach
of winter falling on the
pines

valleys carved a woman
from a child
gave her strength
before she needed
laughter none
could understand
wisdom braided chestnut
mix of briar and vine
locust soldiers
lined the path
from door to gate
nothing there to fear
such a tiny world
slipped between
the orchard
and the wood

unnoticed at the time

I came this way
and made sense
of these
the best I could
looking back and
wondering
if they watched me
as I moved along
into another place
held apart
unseen
might be a memory
remembered
so much clearer
every detail
rich in colors
I never saw them then
in the muted
black and white
flash
before the picture took
time from me
memories pressed
into the space
where none were
meant to be kept
a grey place nestled
quietly
beneath the hope
of red

fell away to nothing

years were
come and went
extravagant their passing
ribbons cut from
honeybees
flowed molasses
through the woods
swift as one could rise
to greet
and fell away to nothing
knew this was the season
and another soon
would be

no more than this
a time and place
unlike the same
another
here to say goodbye
to hold for one more
moment
one more fleeting kiss
taste to
resurrect when nights
forget (there was a day)
what words
would bear repeating
just before as after
precious moments
forsaken to the wrath
of should have been
or might have
was

whatever this
I scarce recall
more than one
of lifetimes spent
ten thousand more
alone and born again
a prodigal commitment
to find this place
of places never known
may not even be
that I might flood
this time
with passionate excess
renaming every wing
restoring faith to
hopeless vine
lost to bloom
the last
relearned the wisdom
found in leaving

come again
and every flower strains
to honor truth
replaced by silver wing
ancient moths
flutter back to see
forgotten everything
the past left
undecided
now welcomes home
another time
for me

sweeter

unwritten page
tells the story
(not confessed)
as secrets freely
whispered
when the night around
us pressed
forever changed
as poems written
on sheets
of consequence
echoed soft in silence
was a (lover's) song
and played again
tones of passion
soft as dew
(midnight falling)
on the blade
and vanished in the heat
of morning sun

if I wondered
of the moments
were passed of this
before
(I could not swear)
that when I kissed you
not a word I tasted there
could have been
redemption cost
unspoken promise
nothing more
verses carried far
(as witness) to the winds
and spoke before

the sweetest words I
know
held much closer to
the dark
and make
no sound at all

I love you
(couldn't wake me)
songs of half-heard
longing (yes)
a melody of something
still
and shifting
invisible
no less
its echo shares
my name

without the promise

wake me up
as starlings rush a morning sky
(unashamed) to beg
the sun into returning
find me where
the road is dirty
lined with silver bells
slippers pink as eyelids
of the whitest one
beyond the dream
(maybe two)
into another place begun
wake me up
when darkness
moves to steal the night
forgotten every
truth we gave away
longing spilled to sheets
without the promise
of another
held to words
were stolen by the moon
eyes still find each other
in the dark
falling into light
(don't take it back)
the sweetest dream
begins anew
when starlings cry
remember love to me
journeys passed
the only proof (I need)

fill my arms with you
wake me up

when the moment came

I wished for more
than I could give
food to feed five thousand more
not only you
your daughter
by your side
wrapped in yesterday
when hope was here
you couldn't see
didn't know this day would come
when hungry
you'd be standing
in the morning rain
I'd see you there
and wonder
when the moment came
what it was
that took you far
from everything
(you loved)
was more than
luck gone bad
or someone not so sure
you'd forgive if he would let you
wasn't meant to hurt
wasn't meant to get you down the way it did
was this the plan
you bought into
long before you held his hand
before this baby girl
wrapped her love around
your heart
of those who pass
you wonder
who can truly see

what do they see
when you give to them to your
smile
your girl says hey
but do they listen
for a moment before they turn away
(they always turn away)
you can't blame them
but for once it might be nice
to have them see
to know they see
(as I can see)
beyond this spell
beyond this place you fell into
might they tell you
of a time (so sure) still to be
when you'll be whole
again
to all you wanted
what you're meant to be
how it is
they've missed you
without missing
when you were always
there

(always here)
I couldn't miss you

not the same

who am I
but love removed
from everything I knew
so used to seeing nothing
but another looked away
what push and pull
of righteousness
together made
for living
before the blur
as eyes were closed
lost when they woke up

I asked a question
waited
for the lies to form
I knew they would
no matter how the others
were
this one to be
the last I'd lose
willed to walk away
wasn't ready
yet to find myself
unwilling to believe

you didn't look away
truth had found me

somewhere else
brought me back
held my hands
(look you said)
listen

how could I believe
when so much is past
between
another life you gave
your promise
then you left
(not the same as leaving)

a heart filled up
with stones
waiting (heavy) with each
choice
to hope again
to come again
remembered
every stone
to float away
might I believe
(as once before)
what you said
before you closed your
eyes

able to return

taken only this
a tiny piece
of all I am
a miracle (unchanged)
to keep inside
how you've been cheated
in returning
what was done
for me
and I for you
saw more than who you were
(were you becoming)
calmer seas
you've never sailed alone
trees that tower
far above
your sleepiness
how could you see
the one you loved
a breath that
wasn't me (starting over)
not even close
saw the rose
dismissing all the red
that was (the sun)
canyons carved
of coral reef
cardinal wings
spread soft against the dawn
held the heavens up
heard the softness of a sigh
never knew the song
(was more
than you could sing)

pools of cappucine

would that I
forgive you of the past
you bring to me
and roses
I could never grow
no matter how it rained
would I take
your breath
and give it back
in summer sighs
would you float
in these pools
of cappucine
forgotten how you got here
whether you can find
your way
or will I hold you
for much longer
than I should
kiss this mouth
and taste the words
I saved for you today
fallen as a whisper
to your tongue
love needs not forgiveness
to begin

faraway places

you sit alone
and just beyond
my tempting touch
a favored place
some things remain
(the same)
familiar look
remembered now
and how I begged
you (come)
from places
(far beyond the yard)
beyond me now
again

were no words to work
or hearth
yet warm enough
to keep you home

(already gone)
I knew
before I knew

I've known you
all along
held you (from a
distance) while
the world a blur
(and you) a vision just as
clear

found me (as I found you)
was not a mystery
I knew would come
forever new
would be
(missing for a while)
a lifetime
(not so long)
more than one
no more to question
death resolved between

we waited
(watching)
wishing for more time
(for sanity)
privy to the stars
we weren't there
when first
they held
our destinies
lonely
hadn't split our hearts
I saw you look
that way

and didn't know
(I couldn't know)
of love
already gone

she who stays

in her darkness
stored as memory
what was done
and what survived
in the shadow of a ring
in moss the smell
of wars returned
(were never won)
living in her bosom
souls of sinners
souls of saints
beneath her lacey
folds
soldiers guard
these pearly gates
demons purged
while we lie sleeping
ghosts her deity
defend
the place she loves
was for us given
gardens lush as green
and old as truth
shall remain
when we have faded
shall remember
her we loved

seasons

if i were the wind
not with a whisper
would i tempt you
but with the silence
of a language
only known by stars
only shared by love
tides tossed and turned
rolled beneath
each passing of the moon
i would show you
seas
beyond this one
but with a look
across the deep
and in the shadows
find you warm
and set to sail

resurrected

with each breath
you restore me
take of these
I have so few
was yesterday I'd
given in
to laughter
(can you hear me still)
when in the night
the dove is silenced
and courage wills
your dreams to come
do you hear
another distant
as the first amen
I spoke
a quietness
as nothing (almost)
head turned
to face the wall
had you not seen
me then
would you have known
(I was)

voice the same
as echoes
laughter disappears
to light
hands that fit
(is nothing quite the
same)
somewhere else
you speak
we're starting over
now

in quiet still
my laughter takes
your breath

come for me

when nights are cold
and beds are bare
when the gale (she moans)
there's no comfort there
might you remember then
what was said to me
when the truth was true
and love was free
when the darkness fills
and storms are passed
when the barn is down
I'll return at last
will you break the seal
of moss to skin
of cross to bone
to relive again
every day we loved
every hope revived
nothing much to keep
only love survives

when the moon is black
stars of long ago
will you look for me
every place you go
will you find these words
(a comfort be)
buried neath the grass
will you come
for me

far away
from now
blows (still)
another wind

thanks giving

permitted this intrusion
into Sunday morning lull
a memory of others
passed
and some I never knew
the holidays upon us
how many gone before
shall we remember
when the plates are passed
and prayer is raised
of all we're thankful for
of children never grown to be
adults they should have been
love that stayed
as others went their way
laughter, loving laughter
chasing down the hall
hands were held
as circles formed
between the chairs
beyond the grave
forgiveness,
tears of coming back
won't recall the time to leave
why it was
and when it ended
will fade as twilight
Christmas trees
where arms are wrapped around
and candles slowly burn
to light the smiles
where love is home
and home is love
despite the world
despite the miles

weeds

won't be long
til most of these I know
will have passed beyond
tomorrow
passed into
the winter snow
the path that led you
to my door
will be covered
by the vines
would keep us from
returning
some orchid choked
by circumstance
the weed
that would be life (still)

I'm okay with that
I can wear a smile
in knowing
this was how we were)
how we came to be (again
we couldn't choose
no choice to be for more
more than a moment
undecided
(take me back)
and let me live again
in places still to be
beside these rivers
(now are running dry)
let me find you there
in meadows I recall
were all we dreamed of
talked about a time or two

and how the stars
would fold into my hair

how ravens danced
circles madly with the moon
wheat and cotton
grew together
for a season came
and we'll remember
I know I will
when everything has gone and only this
the holding on
I will

I will remember
where I left each clue
every word of consecration
every verse (a call to you)
and this believing
this denial of the past
I will find you
as I promised
when first you held my hand
when I first I urged you go
asked no more
than love to stay
you stood against the sun
I watched you melt away
into another place
another life

I will
I will remember

was wandering

what were you looking for
when your eyes
met mine
what were you hoping
still to hear
(when I was whispering)
when touched your hand
what feeling was
a feeling felt before
what kiss was one
(forgotten)
from another time
what path the one you
cleared when we were
younger

(and just wandering)
I wonder
each time I'm taken back
into places I was loved
and love was not enough
nor long enough
easy
to return
the pain of being born
(nothing more)
than will to be
but knowing that the end
will come
before I'm ready
(once again)

I wonder
I'm wandering

where the road will lead
how many to be ended
just to start again
will I hold you long
enough
before I
(will I turn away)
when faced with all I
know
intrigued by what I don't
it brings me back

clinging to a promise
once we made
to find again
the wonder

(was left wandering)
to touch as never
touched
in whispers of hello
(how can I know you)
eyes that reach into
another place we knew
filled with loss
(filled with love
worth dying for)
returning us
again (not soon enough)

I close my eyes
I wonder
I wander

248

purple sash

here am I
beginning
as the stars
upon the grass
as heaven fell
somewhere we meant to
travel
(first was last)
from the edge where
black becomes a
shade of purple sash
before the sun
before the red awakens
here am I
beginning
in the first of words

declared epiphany
in the way a baby cries
a mother knows
the way a father dances
when he's sure no one
can see
the way a girl believes
in something more
a dreams she keeps apart
(more than this she
always knew)
another come to be
for more than she
more than we can be
we are
the place that poets
tell about
a place denied of words

they speak of far away
til we believe

love that needs no
souvenir
(reminders to remember)
hearts that break and
break
(the pain) again
love fills the time
when healing needs to be
and we - we hurry off
in search of something
more
than this for holding
remitted days we wasted
nights we fell apart
(stars upon the grass)
committing now the best
of life
with every goodbye tasted

I've never wished
have never wished to say
I've never known the way
love hurts
what I know is just how
empty life can be
without the hope of love
how many times we
reach
and wakeup empty
how many dreams
undreamed
we still believe

places never kissed

from the time
I first remembered
I've been watching for a
sign
seeking for the reason
I would have come this
way again
(I think I know)
I've felt a strange reprieve
some nights I lie awake
and wonder why I chose
to leave
I press my hands in
prayer
ask God to bless the
same
I read the same ole lines
uttering the same sweet
names
recalled are better days
beneath the maple
spread
quilts and chestnuts
(rolling)
soft across my bed
I remember just how long
the lamp would burn (in
two)
before the night would
win
and soft she'd steal (a
glance) at you
as if you knew her way to
home
did you speak of me

when you were there
alone

I've come this way
remembered this - the
trailing vine
this path (the only
difference)
between your house and
mine

there's nothing here to
show
the back and forth
the coldest nights
the hottest days
as autumn came and
went
south retreated north
and east (just far enough)

there's a tale they tell
and no one really knows
how much we loved
forgotten is the way
I planted flowers every
spring
and how you carried me
that summer
when the locust came to
wing

how we loved
and held (much longer)
for every one we lost

for every moment we
were standing
there were nights we paid
the cost
tho we were left behind
forgotten every notion
how to be
how many broken hearts
before we lost the will to
bleed
did I beg you stay
and all the while rejoicing
in my peace
we hadn't known for
years
we'd made our bed in
tears

was quiet at the table
where we used to sit
one night we stayed up
all night long
laughed and drank a bit
I told you things
I can't believe (I told you
anyway)
of where I'd been
of where I'd fallen
how much I longed to
stay

you held my hand
kissed me
(places never had been
kissed)
whispered in the dark
would we never tire of
this

but we didn't know
couldn't know how hard
the rain would fall
how fragile this old roof
when angry winds were
called
what words we spoke
returning now the need
to know
you turned and I was
glad
to hear the storm door
close

from the time
I first remembered
I've been watching for a
sign
seeking for the reason
I would have come this
way
again
(I think I know)

(I think I know)

251

moments held between

tis never quite enough
the moments held
between
the moment
when you kiss my cheek
the moment that we leave
ripples fall of promise
held
and what will come
when time is come
I watch you from a
distance
but your essence fills
my veins
I wonder what you're
thinking
yet I know the same as
you must know
(can you hear my
heartbeat)
there are no secrets
hidden here
would that I spoke
of longing felt for you
there would be no need
already you know
too much

just because

I saw the words
were just because
a rose was left outside
just off the path
I could have missed it
waiting
thorns remain as beauty
would reveal
I knew was love
and just because
I kept it close
a prickled press
what blood would be
redeemed
or wet my winter coat
held to me
tighter still I pulled it
was just because
I couldn't see
couldn't know for sure
was yours for me
you wouldn't say
I've given up on knowing
what it is you meant
when you left these
words for me
was the rose a gift of
essence
or just thorns
you couldn't keep

snowflakes fell

the rain had fallen
but almost gone
the lights reflecting
in pools of night
and there
I held you
somewhere
when the lonely fell
I tasted them
for moments
just before the chill
was gone
slivers fell of glass
beneath a winter sky
becoming everything
was yesterday
and gone at once
melted into what was then
leaving nothing here
to prove
I've spent my life on
lifetimes
looking for the place they fell
followed every ripple
back to you
looked into the empty night
and never knew
could have been
another snowflake
we were falling for
could have been the only time
the winter wept

another day

was a day like today
and I wished
for another
we could stay
in the shadows
moments undone
as time set aside
for nothing (nothing at all)
whatever would give
to us meaning
you could show me a thing
or two
and I'd show you love
never meant to forsaken
the ways
of just hold me
longing as lullabies played
sunlight waltzed upon us
breaths held
the universe tumbled
sighs counting time
my soul will remember
dreams became reason
(for silence)
words but the echoes
I know

burdened be

from this place
where you've taken me
I can see
quite far beyond
was there a fog I worked
before
walking somewhere
out of sight
to those who might be
watching
and wondered why I was
or what meddlesome
ill I was burdened by
might I be
looking to places
not for me to know
or windows never opened
(let me in)
I walk quietly
feet barely touching
flesh to stone
across floods
and forest floors
waves and willows
what about we were
you can't see
you still wonder why and where
why me
you look into my eyes
and see the fog

unyielding

what questions
I seek (the answers
unyielding)
would peel back the petals
and gaze at the seed
wanting for wonder
another was offered
was not for the taking
when answers came free
and all I was given
was a place for beginning
(a journey) regarded
the first step alone
how far in the darkness
before there is morning
how many the miles
would I walk
until home

you wonder
you ask me
you fade into nothing
you choose
(disregarding) all the lessons unlearned
expect me to know
when your silence speaks louder
than moments becoming
a time long ago

you begged me
beseeching
seek your own savior
choose for believing
from those on your way
what you couldn't know

(I couldn't tell you)
shall find of this coming
a reason to stay
left here to wander
and hailed as a prophet

how long without manna
this longing to fill
what stars to embrace
were no longer shining
what universe passed
is our own standing still

(forgiveness) you never had
to ask why I came
was more than smiles
every sunrise would bring
blue and black ribbons
(halos unfolding)
spread into twilight
bourbon and wing
somewhere
you never expected to find
did the map of your hands
bring you here
(as mine did a lifetime ago)
seeking answers
did the questions take longer
than I did (my dear)
coming again
back to the seeker
what words read aloud
(was purpose decreed)
we heard as a prayer
for salvation
(though silent)
mystery bloomed
from longing (to seed)

for this I was

I've known this way
would be revealed
just how I was never sure
would find in me
the flame I tended
burned sometimes in darkness
meant for this
for this time and place
would rage
to light the corner
would burn to blaze in places
left forgotten (I will not)
I will not let it be
let it be gone or left behind
will not let them
for one moment think
they are nothing more
than nothing
a fallen lilac
a forgotten lily
a gardenia without essence
bloomed without the sun
I will not
leave these wonders to wither
(unknown for their beauty)
the world will know
of what they have lost
will see through different eyes
still
they may turn
but with the weight
of their choice to bear
arms empty of the
sweetest bouquet

rewrite

was not for me you
waited
was yourself
you came to find
read through volumes
saved from some
forgotten
manuscript
you penned before
hung to every word
what memory you'd find
someday
while looking
out beyond the night
the breakers
would sing to you
the truth
ignored at once
and come again
from some other place
another shore
written without reason
but to know that you
would
come
you would walk
these sands
burning feet
and watching for the sun
worried that it might be
set
before you knew

the rest
before you read
the end

if I had told you
would you have
understood
would you have harkened
to my call
would you have listened
when I cried

it's not for me to wonder
not for me to worry out
what reasons were
have found a place to be
tis just enough
for me to be a part
was never mine to keep
or mine to write upon
this your story
your ending to decide
your silence
but a place
to turnaround

where pages might be
blank
you'll know for sure
this your place to be
was not for me
you waited

Jerusalem

would that we choose
the fight (anew)
to burn again
each ancient light
persistent in our right
to be
much greater than the
ten
another who would come
professing loud
the truth
no less for eyes
affixed upon the cross
will only see
the savior (doubt
anointed)
of mortal crown
to reign beneath
a flag of righteousness
forgiven only those would
rise (to disbelief)
would never recognize
(the dream)
Jerusalem

what we keep

she kept it closer
than I would
afraid the thorns
would bruise me
he kept the flame
inside
where only he could
know its warmth
we to choose
and we to burden
others with our
choices
we keep
the worst
sometimes the best
for reasons we alone
can only know
(I can't pretend to know)

held together

from pieces
put back together
someone can make a life
from those we spent
and let time slip away
resolved to find our truth
in ribbons
patchwork notions
threads from one
another grows
vines and paths
across and through
these moments
where we go
touching love
til then another is
and from those words
a song is formed
we sing when no one listens
none can hear our heart
beating (still) out loud
but in the quiet
once we were
believing in forever
held to hands
and searched in eyes
to understand our worth

never knew
the pieces
were the ones we kept
as close as memory
as dear a dream we shared

and gave it life
in telling

when the night was long
and shadows played
on places
where our skin was touching
a place we've lived without
but can't remember
silence when another slept
we watched from by the door
and wept for time
we'd wasted
anticipation

tis all we have
guarded these
the pieces of our hope
trusted when the faith would fail
we'd find the best
still here
fragments ours for holding
when there's nothing else
the echo of a voice
no longer heard
except in passing
stirs within our soul
another time and place
we should have held
onto (for longer)
closed our eyes to capture
what would quickly
fall away

what remains
this day
in pieces
of our love

from the cocoon

the tree stands bare
I like it that way
tiny lights all she needs
to recall
the feel of the dirt
evergreen branches
brothers and sisters
stood tall
she knew
and she knows
what of me is the same
nothing here
would keep me apart
night after night
to dreams I would go
holding still
to a memory of dark
of a place far
familiar
across mountains
to tumble
waking still every day
with the proof
what held me there
in places no longer
no less
than was real
every truth
every layer
of living came back to me
streams cold and clear
just the same

people and pardons
I might have been taken
let not they be marked
with my name
dreams now revealing
colors I never
saw when they first came
to me
spinning in silk
cocoons seeking freedom
wings
but a fond memory

264

backwards into us

were this the end
of moments
come to us
and we could know
where time would leave
us
other worlds
destined for would be
(again)
would then
we understand
just how fleeting life and
love
a dragonfly
on the other side
still a wonder to behold
wings deciding (destiny)
crossing
back and through
the in between
younger older
(as would we remember)
we have no way
to know which way
we choose
until we do
were the end to come
counting backwards
down to one

backward is the coming
was the going
(to return)
a baby to the bed
a star above the rafters
backward falling
mystery
and long nights (still to
pass)
would we see in us
a moment
worth our travels
a path to take
where none have gone
I'll find the night
will find you
near (the end)

ten thousand poppies

when I have taken
all I can
and left not trace
or souvenir
for others who might
pass along
remembering
the way I was
and from a petal fell
(love me not)
upon the wind
to be ten thousand
meadows
scarlet poppies burst
but could not speak
for me
or tell of places
once I was
the place where love
was gifted
held between the hedge
and fences
beneath the arms
where oak and elm
grow to be
together
once more to claim
the place I was
tho taken all I can

when I was falling

seems so much further
this lonely coming back
can't recall
passing here
when I was falling
could have been
that for a moment
I was blinded
by the movement
(snowflakes in my hair)
some flickered
recognition
of the one I was (before)
before I stumbled
you never meant to be
(a place along
the places I was going)
I wonder
how it feels
to breathe again
would I have noticed
when I took you
to a place
(I never knew)

pretty colors

I've wondered
(now I know)
I can't get back
to where I started
seems the distance
(way too far)
and not a day passed
(slowly) by
I'm closer
every flame
(a distant light)
a hopeful moment
I think I've found my way
then a star burns out
and all I see
is darkness
where I thought I was
before
(before you came
to change it all)

is there still a world
(forsaken)
where I haven't found
you yet
I don't recall
a (single) place
you haven't been
a time
without your lingering
shadows into shadows
remembered (where
we were)
and somewhere
I was bound

now another (better)
place
but there's the one
I leave behind
(without these pretty
colors)
tis not a place
I'm gonna find
tis not for me
to wonder

was never meant for me
to find
(my way back)

dreamed in wonderlands

I dreamed in
wonderlands
where rainbows
parted like the sea
archers rode on waves
into the sun
and every wish was
granted
some were given
(more than) room to grow
I knew my place
before the final page
and I would wait
denying every joy
that came between
and carousels
where horses could run
free
I knew them all
(better still) they knew of
me
stories
only I could tell
would save from none
the bliss
beyond the storm

I dreamed in red
the breath of night
against the lacey edge of
day
of summer heat

and winter snows
to take my breath
away
so none would know
I ever was
or saw of this myself
some wonderland
that must have been
reserved for me
to live

I dreamed in lemonade
and cantaloupe
with bitter sauce
of pages willed
to open by my pen
of candles never
threatened
by the run of wax
to wood
I knew of love
the same as of my hand
and made it well
(as it could be)
when passing by my
house

was on the way
to evermore
and stopped
to have a drink

proof that I'm alive

last night
the curtains came apart
and kept me up
past dawn
I cursed the moon
and pulled the blankets
round
(that wouldn't do)
too much of me
was needing of my
dreams
but none would come
shadows held me down
before the rooster rang
I walked a mile
out on the porch
counting boards
where splinters lie in wait
I drank a pot of coffee
might as well
enjoy the view
I waited for the sun
would tell me why
would know
if every dream I had
were gone

was chilly
for a little while

the dew was burned to
frost
could have sworn
that I saw footprints
on the lawn
I heard the barn door
open
were ripples on the pond
reflection of the place
where Venus loved

I heard before I saw it
sliding 'cross
the meadow's blue
crimson fingers begging
me
believe
was blinded by the
brilliance
unlike I'd ever seen
guess I needed proof
I was alive

long before this day is
done
my eyes will beg for sleep
would love to cry
but don't have strength
to grieve

silence hears

what yesterday
I took upon myself to
clear
(again)
forgotten what it was
that made me choose
when I betray
the best of me
another cross to bear
I wonder
when the silence
will grow tired
tis like a lover
warmth surrounds
his arms are opened wide
no need to speak
the name
he knows so well

what happiness
awaits beyond these
pieces I've become
will tears
be shed for me
another day to dry
in making
this amends
have I forgotten how to
live
can speak not of
the past

or what of love
I know

will destiny
be given a place to be
(somewhere)
when debts are paid
and lonely
turns away
will find the hand
was waiting
my tenderness to bear

will I remember
(then)
the price I paid

silence comes
familiar love
to hold me near
again
listens for each
tearful sob released
reminding me
of everything
(love forgot to tell)

I speak your name
but only silence
hears

without a plan

had I known
the last would be the last
the first to leave (for good)
might I have held
a moment longer
than was needed for goodbye
might I have looked into forever
liquid pools where loving burned
oceans where I'd played before
the water (always) warm

might I have kissed
your lips - with urgency
saved for one more day
pulled your heart
(to beat) against my own
trembled in your arms
whispered (don't forget)
might I have begged you
not to go
gave my soul
for just one touch

might I have sailed
into tomorrow
without a plan of where to go
given everything
to hold your hand

would I have noticed
you were melting into
the first of nevermore
the sun no longer
setting in your smile

remember to return

there's an ache
I hadn't noticed
growing deep inside
was longing spilled
amid the flesh and bone
a memory was washed upon
this willing shore
of somewhere else
someone (I can't say)
might have been
the way the moon was wasted on July
the way the loons
had floated (skyward)
was Venus when he turned

I felt the stutter
somewhere
one day I meant to go
was a reflection of the woman
I'd become
I didn't know her then
but have before
was back when I remembered
(I wanted it to be)
before the house came down
before the ribbons flew
and canons took my heart
before you held my hand
my beating drum
begun (again)
before the past was past
someone told me
this would be
the way my life would live
in pieces pulled

long into the night
would linger
over words that had no meaning
(but to me)
would fall between the lines
I never heard

circled now the planets
found the date upon the wall
was today the paper faded
and the flowers fell
I've pulled away the reasons
every lie (I've lost my mind)
I stay up more than sleep
to watch the stars
I know his every face
his steely wonder
he's seen more than he should
but he won't say

it's not for me
to question
not for me to wonder why
(but still I do)
when no one's looking
when I don't have to be so strong
I know the way they fall
every tear I've tasted twice
buried more than one
and saved myself again
stood in distant meadows
burning leaves
my sweet perfume

I've come too far
to choose another mother
brushed from these
the stars out of my hair

Venus

lonely always comes alone
Venus moves aside
holding truth
as hostage
in the place I keep
not a sin
would I confess
no crying for the loss
(I must go on)
pretending nothing changed
when everything
(I know of me)
will never be the same
forever came and went
within a sigh

remembering
the coming back
forgotten now the leaving
the only pain
I couldn't bear
is never to have loved
when nights are passed
will life be kind
and bring you back
to me
or memories betray
the best of us
will moments pass
as whispers I can hardly hear
will Venus come
to steal you once again

wonderful unknowing

so much of the unknown
is in the knowing
wondering how much we
have
and what we have to lose
we plan to win
and plan to fall
and plan to say we never
did
get up and dust
our trousers off
slide our boots beneath
the bed
cry when no one's
looking
dare the world to
disbelief
who of strangers
would ever care to know
we hide the truth
in bottles out behind the
barn
and write on pages
just to watch them burn

we hold within
the only thing worth
keeping
a promise to ourselves
to do one more
to take the chance
to fly the kites

to ride the rails to
Beaumont
to sleep beneath the
milky way
somewhere the midst
of march
to walk naked
through the meadow
bare feet on winter
stones
to swim the cold
when snow is on the
ground
to fill the bucket
more than once or twice

to love like we had
nothing else to do

to live beyond the edges
of this earthly map
to sleep all day
and dance the night with
stars
with dragonflies
to carve our name
with passion to the wood

to love like we had
nothing else
to do

yesterday's winter

yesterday's winter
arrived without grace
flew in from somewhere
I'd forgotten to tell
I thought for a moment
of how it was then
we would dance
while the stars
were deciding our fate
gaze at the moon
in the fountain
sometimes you would
lead me
across cresting waves
was forever we wandered
time and again
believing the notion
this time
would be right
this time would become
the destiny
longed for

so I keep holding back
never give it all up
I want to remember
will return
as I do

when the blackbirds are
blooming
the cicadas
up from the ground
and left us behind a
reminder
of how far we've come
how far to go
starting over
without reason or
memory
picking up scattered
long ago pieces
lockets and lessons
we don't recognize
from before when we held
them
forever so close

last night
the windows were frosted
but to the place
where the winter began

could have been
it was me
coming home

lotus dreams

it's been a while
but only moments
still
I can turn my head
and there
you watching me
there's a whiff
that is your soap
the kind that made your
skin
seem softer than
my own
I would linger there
beneath your ear
caught in webs of
righteousness
drifting on your scent
and listening
the vibration of your
words
spoken something
but who can say
I never heard you say
(it sounded lovely)
but deeper than the well
I fell each time
a little further
was you that saved me
til the next
and like a soldier
to the throne
like a sinner to the altar
like a truth
you couldn't know

I would go
hypnotized by summer
flower
lotus petals on a dream
arms around me
somewhere
else
I wanted them
to stay

a melody I hummed
against the river of your
heart
beating strong against
my voice
taught another song

of lotus dreams
and serenades
I still can't sing
only know them by the
way
they fall
beside me through
the night

lullaby
your essence
makes me sing

dwell in silence

let not this truth
be dimmed
by sorrows come upon
where then the ribbons flutter
as wings against the wind
or give without a lover's rite
to words that had no weight
that had not loved
what good would be
or worth for tears be trade
save all for this
these lonely hands
essence stretched to hold the light
honor made from ash
and flame
burned clean the wick
of life

let not remorse
be mingled with the tongue
that speaks my name
would better dwell in silence
than come to you that way
as something
distant never known
or held against your breast
a petal sailed between
your world and mine
hold fast to truth
as if it were your own to grace
speak softly
when remembering
the best of yesterdays

beneath the snow

speak not of me to love
another would not
understand
of sunlight fell to
shadows
where the weeds were
worn
where blossom merged
with vine beneath the
snow
speak not of worth
or worthiness
I cannot hope acquire
love needs not bed
or bud to have a place
speak not of right
or righteousness
(as if they were the same)
take these my words
and cast them to the
wind
believe with some
uncertainty
the glory of your sighs
give not a night's unrest
to dreams you held a
while
speak not of more than
time forgotten now
what love remains
would not be spoke
to me

a place to lay my head

how many times
I've pleaded
"relieve me of this fate'
how many prayers
negated
by answer
come too late

... too late
and I remembered
what the losing would
reveal
how much of me
the hurt would name
and haunt the lonely
nights
I'd wonder why
then doubt myself
and swear no more
to love
I've given all I had to give
more than more (enough)

tis not for much I wanted
just a place to lay my
head
though wondered
of my karma
gave my heart
my house
my bed

told again the story
changed my mind of how
what end
might find in love
the courage
and the faith
to trust again
the long way back
I never thought
of roads I'd walk anew
of fate I hadn't met
was unprepared
for you

changed the locks

by now
I'm sure you see
(something) more
than I was saying
how many times
you've muddled through
our very last sunrise
some back and forth
of consequence
with no importance now
had I understood
might I have loved you
more

(or less)
...so you would see
my world was changed
as you were walking past
into the only sun
we'd share
some burning light
that covered everything
held onto
(we knew) there'd be no
answers
come for this
we'd choose the best we
could
hold to truth
(we couldn't lose)
I'd change the locks
you'd forget the way
(I was)

... we'd pretend

the past was nothing
more
(than remembering)
before we knew
before the words
were given meaning
before the taste was one
with name
before the planets
(just a place)
where we got lost

had I known you then
(might I have known me
too)
would you have
whispered
always
just to have it said
would I have loved you
then
(or love you even still)
without the need (to
know)
how many lifetimes
passed

...wouldn't miss
the way your eyes
reflected mine
wouldn't change a thing
(of all the things
we couldn't change)
might have been the sun
reminding me
to see

unfinished

it started
the moment
you said you were
finished
what a mess you had
made
being done
were you bored
with the seeking
stoned by re-living
mysteries solved
riddles to love
you become
do they listen
as secrets
you whispered before
how much of the telling
was mine to conceive
mine to remember
of paths
undecided
still I want for a magic
unfinished with me

unpolished
undaunted
unfixed by direction

was what someone said
and you swore not to
hear
you believed
there were reasons
and I believed in forever
saw to the signs
we were written before
and stood aside watching
as years became circles
burned rings into oak
down the road
passed as a star
morphed into sparrows
more than just time
was making it so

when you said
you were finished
I couldn't see how
when so much
the undoing
made no plans to be
done

ash to wing

sometimes
the words are tumbled
burning leaves
as ash to wing
sometimes
were never mine to keep
or mine their worth to
see
I turn them back
pages gilt with gold
if in their ink
your blood be coursed
was not of me
foretold

...were given you
you found them here
you give them life each
day
you choose
for you
the answers come
as written to the clay
tablets carried
from the tomb
you choose
them every time
and from your heart
reflection
of the seeker
(never mine)

it took a while
has taken years
words come back
and time again
always I see (as I see
now)
the truth another keeps
(let go)
the worst of who you are
have courage in yourself
seek not in me your
answers
to fate already dealt
or placed beneath a
lantern
where the future
fears the past
where words become
much more
than words
(you choose) what truth
shall last

Acknowledgements

From the beginning, there was love. For all the forms that it has found its way to me, I am grateful – from the first time I was held by my mother (a baby herself) and my daddy (always my hero), I knew love. I just didn't realize how rich I was from the start.

Thank you for that beginning and all the beginnings I have known since then. Thank you for love that became who I am. Beyond Robert and Bonnie, you are love and a very real reminder of God's plan for the world.

To my brother, Stephen and my sisters, Janey and Renee – you were my very first fans, my dearest friends, and forever a soft place to fall. Of all the gifts I've been given, you are the best. And through you came other branches of love – Daniel, Nathan, Stephen, Andrea, Robert, Stephanie, Hannah, and Cameron. Love remains stronger for every heartache and every loss – the tree spreading to bless the lives of so many (so much).

And, lastly, for Jay, who never gave up and always saw the beauty in my brokenness. I love you. Your love has strengthened me, and graced me with the blessing that is Angi, Kristen and Jay – the presence of Keith and four beautiful grandchildren. Thank you from the depths of my soul.

"When I had no song to sing, you sang to me."